L I G H T
O N
T H E
P A T H

SWAMI MUKTANANDA

PUBLISHED BY SYDA FOUNDATION
A SIDDHA YOGA MEDITATION PUBLICATION

Published by SYDA Foundation
371 Brickman Rd., P.O. Box 600, South Fallsburg, New York 12779, USA

Text designed and typeset by Steve Batliner and Derek Beecham. Production editors: Ed Levy, Pat Donworth, Sushila Traverse, Gail Fairbank-Roch, and Osnat Shurer. Cover design by Cheryl Crawford.

Printed in the United States of America

First published 1972. Third edition 1994

06 05 04 03 02 01 00 99 98   6 5 4 3 2

Library of Congress Cataloging-in-Publication Data
Muktananda, Swami, 1908 -
    [Paramārtha prakāśa. English]
    Light on the path / Swami Muktananda. — 3rd ed.
        p.   cm.
    "A Siddha Yoga meditation publication."
    Includes index.
    ISBN 0-911307-70-2 (pbk.)
    1. God (Hinduism) 2. Self-realization — Religious aspects — Hinduism.
  3. Spiritual life — Hinduism. 4. Gurus. I. Title.
BL1213.32.M8513 1998
294.5'4 — dc21   98-14242
                                                                        CIP

CONTENTS

PREFACE   *v*

INTRODUCTION   *ix*

THE GRACE OF THE GURU   1
    Jnanamarga: *The Path of Knowledge*   2
    Yogamarga: *The Path of Concentration*   4
    Bhaktimarga: *The Path of Devotion*   8
    Siddhamarga: *The Path of the Perfect Ones*   11

THE NATURE OF GOD   25
    Sacchidananda   28
    Jivatman   31

GURU AND DISCIPLE   34
    A True Disciple   38

THE NECTAR OF LOVE FOR THE GURU   45

JAPA YOGA   52
    Mantra: Its Meaning and Potency   56
    Japa in the Four Bodies   63

THE PATH OF KNOWLEDGE   72

SWAMI MUKTANANDA
and the Lineage of Siddha Yoga Masters   84

Glossary   90

Index   95

PREFACE

Every time I open this book, the words evoke indelible memories: Ganeshpuri, India, in 1972, when I met Baba—as we affectionately called Swami Muktananda—for the first time.

This encounter revolutionized my life. I don't know exactly how, or in what precise moment, Baba transmitted his remarkable energy to me. But the day I sat to meditate just after Baba had given me his mantra, I felt a subtle, intelligent power rising from the base of my spine to the crown of my head. My mind became like the surface of a lake untouched by wind—still as glass, without a single thought. In that stillness, a mysterious inner space I'd never experienced before was revealed, and I was that space: clear, pure, and completely content. What surprised me most was that this space was conscious, aware of itself, and of everything around me — it was a space of Light. From that day on, I have wanted to cultivate the serenity of that unfathomable inner landscape.

What had happened? Afterward, I understood that Baba had given me initiation, called *shaktipāt*, which had brought me to the experience of my inner Self. Shaktipat literally means "the descent of energy," and it is precisely the ability to confer this initiation that is the most crucial task of a Guru. Baba himself had received the extraordinary power to awaken the *kundalinī* energy in seekers from his Guru, the great Indian saint Bhagawan Nityananda. According to the Shaivite scriptures often quoted by Baba, this awakening is the most significant event in an individual's life, for

v

over time it leads to the permanent awareness that God is the ecstatic and effulgent core of our being — what the sages and yogis call Self-realization.

After this awakening, though I didn't understand them at first, fascinating things started happening to me in meditation. In those days, Baba seldom gave talks in the Ashram. There were no courses about Siddha Yoga meditation, and the number of books about Siddha Yoga numbered fewer than the fingers on one hand. We spent our days performing the spiritual practices Baba had given us: meditation, chanting, *japa* (repetition of the mantra) and *guruseva*, selfless service to the Ashram. Each was an act of yoga with the uncanny power to clear up our mental dross and bring forth from the inner Light a steady growth of pure love.

From the challenges and striving during his years of spiritual seeking, Baba understood that we would also need a verbal explanation of what was occurring within us. So, once a week, we'd meet on the veranda of Baba's apartment to ask him questions about our spiritual practices and experiences. For the few who lived in the Ashram, and we were under a hundred in those days, this was always the high point of the week—Thursday afternoons when we heard the Guru's teachings. What inspiration Baba had! He would sing from memory verse after verse of the exquisite poetry of India's great saints. His knowledge seemed limitless: he knew the Upanishads and the *Bhagavad Gītā,* the Puranas and the epics of Indian history, Vedanta and Kashmir Shaivism. All these flowed spontaneously from him with a clarity and simplicity that made the ancient teachings utterly relevant.

One of the few written materials we did have with which to study Baba's teachings during this time was a collection of essays that had originally been published in *Shree Gurudev-Vāni,* the Ashram annual magazine. These essays comprise the volume you now have in your hands. In them, Baba speaks to us about the essence of the spiritual journey, the nature of God, and what it means to have a Guru. Baba expresses himself with the language and metaphors of the traditional Masters who have a scholarly grasp of the scriptures and use their knowledge to convey the profound personal experiences that have brought them enlightenment. With the clear understanding of his own inner Light, Baba illumines some of the major aspects of the spiritual path, so that we, too, can follow in the footsteps of the ancient sages.

This new edition retains the original, informative introduction by Swami Prajnananda. A professor of Sanskrit and the first woman to come to live in the Ashram, Swami Prajnananda, known as Amma, was also the first historian of Swami Muktananda's life and teachings. She diligently wrote down Baba's words and his exchanges with devotees and also asked us about our yogic experiences. It was she who assembled these essays into book form over twenty years ago.

Upon reading *Light on the Path* for the first time, what most touched my heart was what Baba had written concerning the grace of the Guru, and how that grace — in the form of shaktipat initiation — is truly the origin of all yogas. In those days a strong undercurrent of love surged in my heart, increasing my devotion for God. I discovered a secret of the path — that it was not the efforts to discipline my mind as much as it was bhakti yoga, my natural love for God in the Guru, awakened by shaktipat, that opened me to the inner realms of meditation. If I had read Baba's essay on the nectar of love for the Guru before receiving the grace of initiation, I don't think I would have either understood or perhaps accepted the tremendous relevance devotion holds toward spiritual growth. By then I had read Baba's marvelous account of his meditation experiences in his autobiography, *Play of Consciousness,* his inspiring exhortations to practice the recitation and study of scriptural mantras in *Nectar of Chanting,* and the few other writings of his that were available in 1972. However, it was in *Light on the Path* that I found the overall delineation of Siddha Yoga meditation and its unique power to bring about the manifestation of the traditional yogic paths such as *jñāna, bhakti, dhyāna,* and *mantra,* solely by the divine inspiration of the awakened kundalini energy.

When this book was published, few people knew what shaktipat was. Since the 1970s, when Baba traveled to different parts of the world, a unique event occurred, unprecedented in history. Literally thousands of people received this initiation and began to have firsthand experiences of the kundalini, as well as the remarkable and spontaneous unfolding of these yogas within themselves. Baba was a pioneer in that he made accessible what for centuries had remained an esoteric secret. These early essays of Baba's are a part of that pioneering work. They are his gift to us all. *Light on the Path* not only conveys Baba's uniqueness as a spiritual Master; it also communicates the importance he always placed on integrating spiritual life with our ordinary, daily life. "To accomplish this inner journey," Baba writes in his characteristically colorful style, "there is no need to abandon your normal pursuits, because daily life in no way hinders the pursuit of God. If this vast, various world were an obstacle to God-realization, then surely God wouldn't have created it. Yet he did create it as a playground for his glory and delight." Baba wanted us to find a practical way to live in the world right now, with the understanding that we are the supreme Light. That supreme Light is the goal; that same Light also guides us on the path.

Although Baba is no longer with us physically, his *shakti*, his divine power, continues to unfold the miracle of the Guru's grace through his illustrious successor and spiritual heir, Swami Chidvilasananda. She continues to bring the grace of shaktipat to all who approach the Guru, searching for a genuine and lasting happiness. The path in itself has never changed. We look back at this early expression of Baba's writings and now see that it contains in essence the enduring teachings of Siddha Yoga meditation. The path simply has become much wider, to embrace all those who long to walk on it.

— SWAMI SHANTANANDA
Gurudev Siddha Peeth
Ganeshpuri, India
October, 1994

INTRODUCTION

Self-realization is the supreme purpose and real meaning of life. When a person suffers from a sense of imperfection or lack of meaning in the material achievements of life, he longs for higher ideals and attainments. He keenly desires a fulfillment that is complete, constant, and indestructible. Such fulfillment is the highest realization.

Several articles by our beloved Gurudev, Swami Muktananda Paramahamsa, explaining the way toward this highest realization are collectively published here for the benefit of seekers. Originally, they appeared in various issues of *Shree Gurudev-Vāni*. They have also been published in Hindi under the title *Paramārtha Prakāsh*.

The article "The Grace of the Guru" contains the essence of Baba's teachings. In it, he discusses the different paths to Self-realization, namely, *jñāna, bhakti,* and *yoga*. Realization can be attained through any or a combination of these paths. However, the path of *gurukripā,* or the grace of a true Guru, is the easiest of all. This path is also known as Siddha Yoga, of which this article is a very comprehensive and lucid exposition. Baba often says, "I am not offering a novel theory or system. I would only like to make you experience in daily life what the great sages have preached and practiced since ancient times." What he means is that the knowledge and realization the saints achieved through severe ordeals can be attained in a spontaneous and natural manner by the grace of a Sadguru. He can reveal to us in an instant what would take a lifetime, perhaps many lifetimes, to attain through our own efforts.

A special feature of Baba's teachings is that he does not consider the world to be unreal or illusory. He describes it as a manifestation of supreme Reality (*brahman*), a projection of *chiti shakti* (divine Consciousness). Just as an artist paints various forms on the same canvas, with the same color and the same brush, similarly Chiti, in its immense joy of self-revelation, bursts forth in different forms and names as well as in different ways, including the thoughts arising in the human mind. Therefore, one need not be frightened or dismayed by the multitude of thought-waves that crowd the mind. One should regard these as a sport of the divine Consciousness because the mind is also one of its pulsations.

Another special feature of Baba's lectures and writings is that they are supported by the words of the scriptures and universally accepted saints, so that listeners and readers may be fully convinced that these are eternal truths.

The article "The Nature of God" is an example of Baba's universal outlook. He says that God-realization is the same for all faiths. All differences are man-made, while God is above all divisions. He is the same for all, whether Hindu, Muslim, Christian, Sikh, Parsi, or Jew. Only one God is the basis of the entire universe.

God has many names, and He can be addressed by any of them. He is with form and attribute, and without. He belongs to all faiths and sects, yet He is above them. The advocates of various religions have tried to describe Him according to their beliefs, but He remains the same — eternal, blissful, and the Truth. In this article, Baba has revealed his profound wisdom of Truth-realization and has described the nature of the supreme Reality as *sat, chit,* and *ānanda* in a way that seekers will easily understand.

In the article "Guru and Disciple," the nature of the grace-bestowing Guru is explained. A real Master is the embodiment of God's divine power. Having fully merged with God, he is His manifestation in physical form. Only such an enlightened soul is capable of bestowing grace on deserving aspirants. By the light of his ever-shining Spirit, the Guru touches and awakens the "sleeping" soul of his beloved disciple, and then the light of that highest Spirit also begins to shine in the disciple. One lamp is lighted from another lamp. This is known as *shaktipāt*. A disciple can receive this great gift through single-minded devotion, total love, and constant service to his Guru. In short, the only key to attaining the Guru's grace is complete devotion to the Guru.

The theme of the article "The Nectar of Love for the Guru" is that a seeker who loves his Guru wholeheartedly and with complete devotion is able to see God embodied in his Guru. He who has tasted the nectar of the Guru's love feels his entire world to be fully merged with his Master. He does not have even the slightest attachment to any external thing or person. Baba says that the bliss, beauty, and enlightenment resulting from intense love for the Guru can be known only through experience. It cannot be adequately described. Thus, this article is a superb account of what a disciple can achieve by following the path of the Guru.

The article "Japa Yoga" explains how repetition of the mantra given by a Siddha Guru can also lead to the attainment of divine grace. This, too, is a form of Guru's grace. When the live mantra given by the Guru is repeated constantly, it descends from the tongue to the throat, from the throat to the heart, and from the heart to the navel. When this fourth stage is reached, repetition of the mantra becomes automatic. The unique process of *japa yoga*, which is borne out by actual experience, is described in detail in this article. Not only does it explain what is stated in the scriptures, but it also gives us firsthand knowledge of Baba's own rare experiences.

"The Path of Knowledge," which Baba wrote in Melbourne, Australia, adds the personal touch of his own example to the illuminating exposition of this path. In this article, Baba makes it clear that ultimately it is knowledge that dispels ignorance and brings salvation. Without knowledge, everything, including *japa, tapa*, silence, worship, and even meditation, is useless. But this knowledge does not manifest within oneself without *gurukṛipā,* and for that, *guruseva,* or service to the Guru, is necessary.

Baba is one of the few living Gurus who is an adept in *shakti-pāt dīkshā.* Those who have received his grace know that he has, by his living touch or glance, lighted the divine flame in many a pure-hearted and longing seeker. When a seeker receives shakti-pat, he experiences an overflowing of bliss within and becomes ecstatic. Thus, by his divine power, Baba makes the seeker realize his true nature by giving him the experience of divinity within his own Self. In Baba's presence, all doubts and misgivings vanish, and one experiences inner contentment and a sense of fulfillment. The awakening of the divine energy through shaktipat manifests in various interesting ways. Some people hear melodious music within. Others see the Guru in the form of their chosen deity or some other god. Some see the Guru even if they are thousands of miles away and receive personal guidance from him. Some get a glimpse of their past lives.

There is such unique power in Baba's grace and such love in his personality that even his spoken or written words have great force and appeal. Many people have gone into deep meditation and experienced joyful peace while reading his words with complete absorption.

This collection of Baba's articles is being published with the hope that it will light the path for many who have sincerely embarked on the journey toward God.

—SWAMI PRAJNANANDA (AMMA)
Gurudev Siddha Peeth
Ganeshpuri, India, 1972

CHAPTER ONE

THE GRACE OF THE GURU

What is the ultimate goal of life and how can it be attained? Since ancient times the Hindu scriptures have expounded this theme. The seers of profound wisdom have said that to be entirely rid of pain, suffering, and sorrow and to attain the full measure of absolute bliss is the real goal of all beings.

Not only human beings but all creatures on this earth, from the tiniest to the largest, seek happiness and pleasure. Everyone strives in different ways for happiness, peace, plenty, and joy. It is for happiness that we manage factories and other enterprises, build houses, plant gardens, and raise families. For the same reason we pursue various arts, watch dramas, dress up, and enjoy feasts. In every aspect of daily life, our quest is for happiness. Thus, happiness is the real goal of a person's life.

Really speaking, in all these things we are seeking lasting happiness, but we do not know where and how to find it. The actual attainment of ceaseless, eternal bliss, which can be obtained by entering the realm of transcendental joy, is described as *moksha,* or God-realization. This is true religion. Religion is realization, and truly this is the highest purpose and ultimate goal of our life. It is true that we can experience supreme bliss in our own being, that we can realize the very essence of existence within and even transform our being into that highest essence. Therefore, it can be said that the attainment of supreme bliss is the highest goal of all human endeavor.

There are various means and systems in the world for attaining this goal. Different religious paths and philosophical systems have been enunciated by great seers. *Jñāna, yoga, bhakti* and the path of the Siddhas based on *gurukripā*, the grace of the Guru, are chief among them. These paths are closely allied, yet each is singularly perfect and complete in itself. All religions, all paths, and all sects belong to the one Supreme Being and ultimately lead to Him alone.

JNANAMARGA
The Path of Knowledge

Knowledge is one of the means of attaining God-realization. It is knowing one's real Self by acquiring knowledge of the Truth in its essence through the teachings of a Guru. According to the *Bhagavad Gītā*, the *Brahma Sūtras,* and the Upanishads, the *chaitanya ātman*, or conscious Self—which pervades everything without any distinction whatsoever, which is the sole support of everything, which having no support other than itself is ever perfect in itself and is self-existent, which, though residing in all the various types of bodies, does not assume those bodily forms, and which without changing its own true nature exists in everything as its own Self—is itself the indwelling soul of every being. That is the adorable Purushottama, the highest of all beings.

The *Vimarshini,* a commentary by Kshemaraja on the *Shiva Sūtras,* defines *chaitanya ātman* as:

chetayate iti chetanaḥ
sarvajñānakriyāsvatantraḥ
tasya bhāvaḥ chaitanyam.

That which imparts consciousness and possesses an independent power of creation as well as knowledge of all kinds—its state is known as *chaitanya.*

That ever-shining *chaitanya,* which is completely different from the insentient, enters all things and brings them to life, and although it assumes their various forms, it always remains intangible. It is *alinga* (without any mark whatever) and therefore unknowable. It is all-pervading, although it is not visible to those without the eye of wisdom. It has neither hands nor feet, yet it firmly holds all the elements of the universe and travels everywhere. Sitting in perfect steadiness, it proceeds afar to all quarters. To see without eyes and to speak without a tongue are its amazing glory and greatness. With the winking of its eyes, the creation and dissolution of the whole universe occur. Although it is ever present in its fullness in the hearts of all human beings, it is imperceptible to those who have not earned the grace of the Guru; that is, it remains concealed. That highest *chaitanya* is *sacchidānanda* (existence, consciousness, and bliss), which in Vedanta is described as the ultimate goal of life.

In short, the *chaitanya,* which imparts consciousness to all yet remains aloof and absolutely independent, is itself the various deities, and it alone is the supreme Lord; truly, it is the *ātman,* or Self, seated in the hearts of all living creatures. To know the *ātman* through hearing (*shrāvana*) and repeatedly reflecting on the teachings of the Guru (*manana*), and then to become one with it through the practice of meditation (*nididhyasana*), is the way of *jñānis,* or followers of the path of knowledge.

While realizing the *ātman,* a few truly fortunate ones instantaneously become identical with that infinite, universal *chaitanya,* in which they merge and melt their individualities, or their finite selves. This is like a droplet of water becoming an ocean by losing its name, form, and identity in the vastness of the ocean. But this comparison is inadequate, because the droplet of water loses name and form, while the *ātman* neither loses or abandons name and form, nor regards them as unreal; by merging in Consciousness it merely transforms finite self into infinitude. That is, a seeker, pursuing the path of knowledge as taught by the Guru, merges his consciousness into the all-pervading Consciousness and thereby establishes his identity with that *chai-*

tanya. Subsequently, he goes on repeating "I am That, I am That" (*So' ham, So' ham*), and also "I am the All; all are mine." His "I" and the "All" become identical. Thus, the *jñāni* reaches a state in which he becomes free of all distinctions such as internal and external, in which he is without the sense of many and one, and in which his Self experiences unity in diversity. Aloof from all, he attains perfection. Seers, the wise ones, have described this state as *turīyātita* or *nirvikalpa*, which is beyond anything that could be expressed in words and which is no different from the state of unity between *jīva*, the individual soul, and Brahman, as visualized by the preceptors of the Advaita philosophy in the well-known statement (*mahāvākya*) from the *Yajur Veda*, "I am Brahman" (*Aham Brahmāsmi*). This is nothing but Vedanta. In the end, the absolutely unrestricted supreme bliss of oneness is obtained on this path. After attaining divine bliss, the human soul rises above the ordinary feelings of pleasure and pain and remains unaffected by those transient states. After hearing all this, one may feel that through the path of knowledge it is quite easy to attain Self-knowledge, but in actual practice it is extremely difficult and attainable only by great effort and continuous endeavor. Nevertheless, one who is prepared even to be hanged or crucified for the sake of the Truth tastes the divine nectar and attains immortality. The *Shvetāshvatara Upanishad* (I:11) says:

jnātvā devam sarvapāshāpahāniḥ.

Through knowledge of God, all fetters are destroyed.

YOGAMARGA
The Path of Concentration

Another means of attaining God-realization is *yoga*. Restraining the thought-waves that are continuously formed and modified in the mind is known as yoga. The word "yoga" comes from the Sanskrit root *yuj*, "to unite"; therefore, yoga also means uniting oneself with the Universal Consciousness. According to the Maharishi Patanjali, one can achieve this by practicing eight phases of yoga, namely, *yama, niyama, āsana, prāṇāyāma, pratyāhāra, dhāraṇā, dhyāna,* and *samādhi.*

In this path of yoga, following *yama, niyama,* and other successive courses of discipline, one gathers together all one's scattered vital energies, both mental and physical, and brings them under one's control to achieve steadiness of the mind. As soon as the mind becomes calm and steady, an abundance of joy arises in the heart of the aspirant. This is the same as attaining the blissfulness described in Vedanta. Ultimately *jñāna,* knowledge, becomes *yoga,* union. It can also be explained in this way: *jñāna,* which means knowing the Self as none other than the Supreme Reality, is the same as *yoga,* which means uniting the individual self with the Universal Consciousness, eternally pure, illumined, and ever free. This being so, Lord Krishna says in the *Bhagavad Gītā* (V,4-5):

> *sānkhyayogāu pruthag bālāḥ pravadanti na panditāḥ;*
> *ekamapyāsthitaḥ samyag ubhayor vindate phalam.*
> *yat sānkhyaiḥ prāpyate sthānam tad yogairapi gamyate;*
> *ekam sānkhyam cha yogam cha yah pashyati sa pashyati.*
>
> It is the ignorant and not the wise who speak of *jñāna* and *yoga* as different. He who is rightly established even in one wins the fruit of both. The goal that the followers of *jñāna* attain is also reached by the yogis. He sees truly who sees both *jñāna* and yoga as one.

These words clearly explain that the final attainment is the same whether one follows the path of knowledge, which is a direct approach to Self-knowledge as propounded by Vedanta, or the path of yoga, which is a method of reaching the *nirvikalpa samādhi* through the practice of eightfold yoga.

Maharishi Patanjali formulated a very important work on the science of yoga called the *Yoga Sūtras.* Patanjali is considered the highest authority on yoga, and the book, also known as *Yogadarshana,* is prescribed as a text for the systematic study of yoga. In a few aphorisms, Patanjali gives very useful directions for all spiritual aspirants. The *Yoga Sūtras* do not contain theories that involve intellectual reasoning or controversial disputes; they are simply a practical treatise on the science of yoga.

This practical aspect of yoga first of all helps to make the body physically fit and strong by purifying its basic constituents. One may ask why so much importance is given to the body. I would say that a healthy body is absolutely essential for the practice of yoga. It is said that the body is the first and foremost means of practicing religion: *sharīramādyam khalu dharma-sādhanam.* How can one be happy or feel comfortable if the body is sick or weak? How is the practice of religion or any form of spiritual discipline possible for such a one? Therefore, in the beginning, the very practical science of yoga not only emphasizes this point, but is even capable of making the human body strong and sturdy, provided that the instructions are strictly carried out. In the end, it elucidates in detail how, in the state of *samādhi,* one can attain an irrevocable union with the pure, undifferentiated Consciousness. The path of yoga is complete in itself. Even so, one is earnestly advised to have a teacher for proper guidance.

The third aphorism of the *Yoga Sūtras* is *tadā drashtuḥ svarupe'vasthānam,* "At that time, the aspirant will be established in his own true nature." This is the highest fulfillment of yoga. When, after repeated attempts at concentration, a yogi succeeds in bringing all the modifications of the mind under control, he sees his own true nature and attains perfection, or supreme blessedness. To attain and to be established in one's own real nature is the reward that yoga grants to the yogi. In the *Bhagavad Gītā* (VI,46), the Lord commands, *tasmād yogī bhavārjuna* — "Therefore, O Arjuna, become a yogi." For this reason, it can be said that even the Lord is in favor of the practice of yoga.

Besides Maharishi Patanjali, there were other seers, such as Vyasa, Yajnavalkya, Kapilmuni, and Shvetashvatara, who wrote on the unfathomable subject of yoga. The attainment of *yogā-nanda,* the bliss one experiences when united with God in a state of *samādhi* achieved through the practice of concentration and meditation, is the main objective of yoga.

Many people are frightened by the idea of yoga. They believe that yoga is meant for those who renounce their households and live in a jungle or a cave, subsisting on roots or tubers. This conception is entirely false. In fact, yoga is an admirable way of life to be followed without fear by everyone in the world.

All intelligent people, even if they are householders, can practice yoga because it does not deny them a modest and rational worldly life. In fact, yoga is complementary to such a life and, in time, becomes a friend to it.

Actually, the eight constituents of yoga are already being practiced, at least in part, in daily life. For example, *yama* and *niyama* in a broad sense mean the observance of certain rules of conduct. *Āsana* means sitting in a particular posture. *Dhyāna* means concentration. Are not rules and regulations observed in worldly life? Does one not sit in a proper manner? Can an artist, a sculptor, a watchmaker, or an engineer perform his work properly without concentrating and without forming an image of the final product before his mental eye? Can anyone be crowned with success without planning anything in the mind at the outset? Without steadying his mind, can a student concentrate on his studies or pass his examinations? Can anyone have a sound sleep without making the mind free of thoughts and anxieties? Of course not. Yoga teaches us the same things: how to concentrate, how to make the mind steady and free of thoughts, and how to train and cultivate the mind in order to become absorbed in a goal. The instances given above very clearly show how the different parts of yoga are used or practiced in daily life. Nor is this practice limited to the physical and mental planes alone. It extends as well to the moral aspect. *Satya,* one of the moral disciplines, means truthfulness. Is not a wife truthful and loyal in her dealings with her husband? Is she not always honest with him?

Nowadays, many hospitals are filled with the sick. Why? The primary reason is that most people today lead a disorderly and irregular life. Those who lead a life in conformity with the rules laid down in the science of health are immune to suffering and paying visits to physicians. A sound body and good health are of utmost value. They are real wealth. Regular habits and a balanced way of life are yoga put into practice. Yoga teaches these regulations and a way of life that is very conducive to good health. Thus, yoga chases away all one's weaknesses. It creates heaven on earth by transforming all ugliness into celestial beauty. Yoga is therefore a peerless friend of both the worldly-minded and the spiritually inclined. It should be practiced daily, regularly, and with respect.

BHAKTIMARGA
The Path of Devotion

Intense love of God is known as *bhakti,* or devotion. Like *jñāna* and *yoga,* *bhakti* is a means to God, perfect in itself. The way of love is the sweetest, like nectar. *Premānanda, pūrnānanda, yogānanda, sacchidānanda, brahmānanda* — all these terms convey the same meaning, namely, the enjoyment of perfect bliss. On attaining Self-knowledge, the *jñāni* comes to realize that the entire world, full of movable and immovable entities, is nothing but the manifestation of the one Supreme Reality. Knowing this, he becomes free from all duality, such as pain and pleasure, love and hate, likes and dislikes. Then within his innermost Self he becomes the subject of perfect bliss and is ecstatic. When a yogi, through the practice of *yama, niyama, prānāyāma,* and *dhyāna,* succeeds in attaining the state of mindlessness, he experiences the same supreme bliss that the *jñāni* experiences through Self-knowledge. Thus, the yogi is intoxicated by *yogānanda,* the *jñāni* is absorbed in *jñānānanda,* and similarly the *bhakta* becomes enraptured in *premānanda.* This is the ecstatic delight of love of all the love-stricken devotees of God.

The goal may seem to differ because the approaches are different in the paths of *jñāna*, *yoga*, and *bhakti*; but this is not so, for even *bhaktas* love and adore the eternal, imperishable, perfect Brahman alone. In the *Shrīmad Bhāgavata Purāna* (X ,14, 32) it is said:

> *aho bhāgyamaho bhāgyam nandagopavrajaukasām;*
> *yanmitram paramānandam pūrnabhrahma sanātanam.*

Oh, how great is the fortune of Nanda and the other cowherds living in Vraja, since Lord Krishna, the imperishable, perfect Brahman, full of bliss, is their friend.

Is there a place or a person without love? How can there be love where there is no *rasa* (essence of joy)? The very core and nature of God is love, bliss, and ecstasy. The *Taittirīya Upanishad* (II,7) says, *raso vai saḥ; rasam hyevāyam labdhvā' nandī bhavati,* "Truly God is *rasa* and truly, on obtaining the *rasa*, one becomes blissful." The *Taittirīya Upanishad* further says (III, 6):

> *ānandād hi eva khalvimāni bhūtāni jāyante,*
> *ānandena jātāni jīvanti,*
> *ānandam prayantyabhisamvishanti.*

All these beings are indeed born from bliss; being born they live by bliss, and after death they enter into bliss.

It is from bliss that the world is created, maintained, and destroyed. That God Himself is the cause of creation was unequivocally accepted by the philosophers who founded the six systems of Indian philosophy. The cause (God) is inseparably entwined with its effect (creation). From all this, it is clear that love is the original cause or source of creation, for one grows by love, lives by love, and finally even merges into eternal love. Love is all-pervading. To aspire to the Divine would, therefore, mean to love the Divine.

Knowing his beloved God to be present everywhere and seeing Him in all things, a *bhakta* leads his life happily and contentedly. Such a devotee creates a veritable heaven wherever he happens to be. Whatever is seen by the eyes, the lover perceives as his charming Beloved; whatever is heard by the ears, the lover recognizes as the gentle voice of the Beloved. With his tongue he continuously chants the sweetest melodies of love in praise of the Beloved, and his entire body feels the softest touch of his Beloved. A drop of water in the midst of an ocean beholds nothing but water on all sides. Similarly, a *bhakta* perceives God everywhere and rejoices. How does one gain such sight and such joy? The means to behold Him in this way are the incessant singing of devotional songs and rendering of loving service, which are made possible by merging the entire heart and mind, together with the intellect, ego, and senses, with the Beloved. Immortal joy is the final achievement.

This immortal joy can, however, be obtained only by the grace of great souls. In *Narada Bhakti Sūtras* (39) it is said:

mahatsangastu durlabho'gamyo'moghashcha.

The company of the great is incomprehensible, infallible, and difficult to attain.

It is not easy to come in contact with such beings, and it is even more difficult to be a recipient of their grace. Nevertheless, without the grace of a man of God, a devotee cannot become a true lover of God. Through direct contact with godlike saints and their loving influence, the path of love can become easy.

So far, we have seen three different ways of attaining the ultimate goal of Self-realization: *jñāna, yoga,* and *bhakti.* A person can reach his spiritual goal by the practice of one or all three of these means. Although these paths differ from each other, the spiritual aspirants of each one can arrive at the same goal and attain the same immortal state. But these means are very difficult and wearisome, because one has to suffer a great deal of hardship before attaining liberation and supreme bliss. The *Katha Upanishad* (I, 3. 14) says:

kshurasya dhārā nishitā duratyayā
durgam pathastatkavayo vadanti.

Sages declare that the path is difficult and hard to traverse, like the sharpened edge of a razor.

The road to supreme knowledge is extremely narrow, and it is compared to a razor's edge. The path is so arduous that one Hindi poet says it is like chewing peanuts made of steel. The Lord Himself says in the *Bhagavad Gītā* (VII, 19) that even a *jñāni* attains the state of supreme bliss only after the hard work of many lives:

> *bahūnām janmanāmante jñānavān mām prapadyate.*

A *jñāni* attains Me at the end of many births.

This being the case, a seeker may wonder whether there is any other way to the final goal besides these three. There is indeed a way. It is an easy discipline that one acquires from a Sadguru. If he is gracious and his kind favor descends upon a seeker, the entire path of *sādhanā* becomes simple, comprehensive, and effortless. It is known as the path of the Siddhas.

SIDDHAMARGA
The Path of the Perfect Ones

This easiest and surest means to the goal is also known as *gurukripā*, the grace of a perfect Master. By the grace of a Sadguru, a true and earnest disciple turns an inaccessible path of *sādhanā* into an easy way to proceed on the spiritual journey. Once he has been initiated by the Sadguru, his path is automatically rendered smooth, clear, and easy to practice.

Shaktipat Diksha

In every sect or religion there is a tradition of *dīkshā*, or initiation. The real meaning of *dīkshā* is "to give" — to give an awakening whereby the initiated one can have a superconscious vision of the Lord and ultimately experience his identity with that Supreme Self.

The grace of the Guru is itself a process of initiation known as *shaktipāt dīkshā*. This is the same process of grace whereby Shri Ramakrishna Paramahamsa gave a direct experience of divinity to Swami Vivekananda the moment he touched him. Indeed, the process of *shaktipāt dīkshā* is highly mysterious, secret, and amazing. It is a very ancient tradition practiced in India. The following are three typical illustrations of *shaktipāt dīkshā:* (1) the bestowing of grace by means of which Shri Gahininath, in an instant, made Shri Nivrittinath realize the highest Brahman; (2) the transmission of divine shakti that happened when Kabir Sahib was accidentally touched by Shri Ramanandaji and which brought about within Kabir a spontaneous awakening of intense love and devotion for God; (3) the secret process by which Shankaracharya, just by casting a glance at Hastamalaka, made him a knower of the Self. The first illustration is one of *manasa dīkshā* (by the will of the Sadguru), the second is of *sparsha dīkshā* (by the touch of the Sadguru), and the third is of *drik dīkshā* (by the glance of the Sadguru).

Swami Shankar Purushottam Tirth, the Shankaracharya of Govardhan Math, knew its secret and was thoroughly proficient in initiating by *shaktipāt dīkshā*. His book *Yogāvanī* (written in Bengali and in Hindi) is an authentic treatise on the subject. In the *Gheranda Samhita, Vayaviya Samhita, Skanda Purāna, Kulārnava Tantra, Yogini Tantra, Agama Sandarbha, Sharada Tilaka,* as well as in the books of the Shaiva, Vaishnava, and Saura paths and in certain yogic Upanishads, the subject is dealt with fully. Even among the *lamas* of Tibet this is a customary practice, but not everyone is familiar with it. People with partial and superficial conceptions do not know the subject well enough, and they err.

Mahaprabhu Shri Gauranga, out of his divine mercy and love, even initiated several bad characters like Nauroji, a notorious thief, and Lakshmibai and Satyabai, two courtesans. After Shri Gauranga Prabhu aroused divine love in their hearts, they turned toward God and spent the rest of their lives in devotion.

There are those who doubt the efficacy of *shaktipāt.* Some deluded people misinterpret it as a tantric *sādhanā.* This is sheer ignorance. Others think that it is either a practice of *vāma marga,* the left-handed path, or a mode of worship of Shakti which is not considered valid by the scriptures. Being misinformed, though erudite scholars, they are on a false path and do not know the slightest secret of *shaktipāt.* On hearing the word *shakti,* they presume it has something to do with *shaktas* (worshipers of Shakti) and thus remain far away from true God-realization. For countless ages, *shaktipāt* has been used as a secret means of initiation by the great sages. To transmit one's own glory and luster of divine enlightenment into a disciple and give him an instantaneous, direct experience of Brahman, the Eternal Spirit, is the secret meaning of *shaktipāt.*

To explain this, I will narrate a true story. In Marathawada, there is a town named Ambajogai, a place of pilgrimage famous for its temple Jogai-ki-Amba. Once Jaitrapal, the ruling king of the region, went on horseback to a yogi named Mukundrai and insisted that the yogi show him the Supreme in the short time required to mount a horse with one leg already in the stirrup. At this obstinacy, by one slash of the king's own whip, Mukundrai made the king realize the Supreme Reality. By the power acquired through austerities, sages can either bless or curse. In the same way, it is neither impossible nor difficult for them to transmit spiritual energy to a disciple on the strength of their divine knowledge. It is bound to be experienced by earnest and sincere aspirants on the spiritual path.

In every human being there dwells a divine energy, the *kundalinī shakti.* This energy has two aspects: one manifests *samsāra,* the ephemeral worldly existence; the other leads to the highest Truth. When the Guru transmits his soul power to a disciple, the latter aspect of the Kundalini Shakti is automatically activated in the disciple and set into operation. This is known as *shaktipāt dīkshā* or *gurukripā.*

That energy, which has the supreme capacity to create the universe independently, is called *chiti shakti.* This pure Consciousness, which is full of absolute bliss, dwells in the Guru in its full-ness. Assuming the three different aspects of unity, diversity, and unity in diversity, creating the universe of manifold forms out of one, and manifesting many in one and one in many, Chiti Shakti reveals an ever-changing world in the *ātman*, which is a changeless reality. This active energy has many names—Chiti, Mahamaya, Shiva's Gauri, Narayana's Lakshmi, Rama's Sita, Krishna's Radha, the yogi's Kundalini, the poet's inspiration, and the blissful stream of joy of the *ātman*—and an infinite number of aspects. This divine energy is not in any way different from or independent of the highest Reality. Both the Reality and its divine energy are one and the same, just as a king and his ruling power go together.

When the attributeless, formless, changeless Reality which underlies the entire universe, and which is the pure, ultimate Consciousness, is stirred up, this divine energy begins to operate in it. She is the power of becoming, released out of the Eternal Being and expressing herself through all names, all forms, and all changes that we call the world. Indeed, She is the most magnifi-cent power—Shri Kundalini Shakti—of the Supreme Reality. To set this Kundalini into operation within an individual being is known as *shaktipāt*, and one who gives *shaktipāt dīkshā* is a Guru. The *Yoga Vāsishtha* says:

> *darshanāt sparshanāt shabdāt*
> *kripayā shishyadehake;*
> *janayedyaḥ samāvesham*
> *shāmbhavam sa hi deshikaḥ.*

> He who, by his gracious look, touch, or word, gives to the disciple an experience of his identity with the Absolute is indeed the Guru.

In the *Kulārnava Tantra* it is said:

> *guroryasyaiva samsparshāt*
> *parānando' bhijāyate;*
> *gurum tameva vrunuyāt*
> *nāparam matimānnarah.*

A discriminating person should choose as his Guru none else but one by whose touch he experiences the highest bliss.

Experiences of the Awakened Kundalini

After a disciple is initiated by such a Guru, various types of internal activities occur. Some disciples experience great joy, while others become either apparently dull and stupefied, or restless. With certain disciples a variety of strange bodily reactions, such as yogic postures, gestures, tremors, or dancing poses, begin to take place involuntarily in every part of the body. This may cause wonder. Some disciples get frightened. For a short period of time, one may feel pain in almost every part of the body. Various stirrings may occur in the heart, head, and abdomen; and throbbing of the muscles and fascinating, thrilling sensations may be experienced. One may feel drowsy and may even enter a state of deep meditation without making any effort. When a disciple begins to see lights of different colors—red, white, black, and azure—in meditation, his joy increases day by day, and he follows his spiritual discipline with greater enthusiasm. Sometimes during meditation one may see temples, mountains, caves, and even other worlds. Thereafter, a divine light of indescribable luster is always visible during meditation. That light is considered to be the light of the qualified, or manifested, Reality (*saguna brahman*). The *Pashupata-brahma Upanishad* describes it in this way:

> *akalpitodbhavam jyotih svayam jyotih prakāshitam;*
> *akasmād drushyate jyotis tajjyotih paramātmani.*

The light does not appear by any pre-imagination, but is manifested by itself. Such self-resplendent light is seen unexpectedly during meditation. The light which thus makes itself evident exists in the Supreme Self.

Other worlds are also seen in this divine light, and the disciple comes to know that *pitruloka* (the world of the ancestors), *chandra-*

loka (the world of the moon), and *devaloka* (the world of the gods) actually exist.

Various emotions (*ashtabhāva*) may be automatically awakened. Overwhelmed, the disciple swims in an ocean of infinite bliss, filled with joy and delight. Day by day, as his zeal and fervor increase, the disciple has countless experiences. With each new vision and divine experience, his steadfastness and enthusiasm in the practice of discipline grow, which helps him to continue with added vigor. If he follows the proper rules of conduct, such a seeker may carry out his daily routine or worldly dealings, may visit and stay in any part of the country, and yet, due to his intense faith, see and feel the presence of his adorable Guru everywhere. Be assured that this is no myth, nor am I writing about magic. Rather, it is an unmistakable fact that the Supreme Spirit is truly and eternally all-pervasive and has penetrated every atom of the visible universe. This Self, as Consciousness, permeates the entire world of the animate and inanimate, sentient and insentient. This is explained in the *Shiva Sūtra Vimarshini*:

> *tadeva bhavati sthūlam sthūlopādhivashātpriye;*
> *sthūlasūkshmavibhedena tadekam samvyavasthitam.*
>
> O beloved, That itself becomes the gross by conditioning itself into the gross. That alone exists in the different gross and subtle entities.

Just as the Universal Consciousness (Chiti), by limiting itself, becomes the individual consciousness (*chitta*), similarly the sentient (*chetan*) changes itself to appear insentient (*jada*). That is, the highly luminous Self, while manifesting itself as gross entities, becomes conditioned and limited in the form of diverse objects. The pervasive Self becomes the pervaded. Therefore, the pervaded is not separate from the pervasive because the pervader and the things pervaded by Him are the same, not different. I am reminded of a saint's poem:

Whether I call you an earring or an anklet,
  a brooch or bracelet,
The inherent gold glitters brightly in you.
So is the Self seen shining through everything.

There are other analogies that explain this. The physical body, heterogeneous as it is, is formed from one drop of semen. Throughout cotton fabric, there is nothing but cotton threads; in the fabric there are threads, and in the threads there is cotton. Similarly, the Lord, the Supreme Spirit, is the basis of everything, including the movable and the immovable entities of this universe. Therefore, the universe itself is the cosmic Self.

I will give one more illustration. A steamer leaving the Bombay dock is on the sea until it reaches the port of Mangalore. The steamer is not at any moment separated from the sea. In the same way, aspirants who have been initiated by *shaktipāt* dwell in that one Universal Consciousness — Chiti — whether they carry on their spiritual practices at one end of the world or the other. It is therefore not at all surprising if they see their Guru or their chosen deity in visions even when they are thousands of miles away, because just as the steamer is always in the water until it reaches the port, so also the indwelling *chaitanya* is always with aspirants in all places, at all times, and under all conditions. *Chaitanya* is uniform everywhere because it is all-pervading. All this is absolutely true.

In the *Tantrasāra*, it is said that the Lord's Shakti is full of infinite wonders: *tacchamatkāra icchāshaktiḥ*. It is She who wills various yogic processes in *sādhakas* (seekers). Then an array of wonderful yogic *āsanas*, *mudrās*, and different types of meditation take place. These yogic exercises cleanse the nervous system. Generally, by the process of *nāḍīshuddhi* (purification of the subtle channels within the body) many diseases and ailments are cured. Many types of *prānāyāma* are also performed automatically. These open up all the *chakras* (psychic nerve centers), and thus, in a very simple and easy manner, the passage in the *sushumnā* is cleared of all obstructions. The *prāna* rising through the *sushumnā* is stabilized upon reaching the *sahasrāra*, the spiritual center at the crown of the head. This process of *nāḍīshuddhi* goes on until the *prāna* and *apāna* are finally equalized. It is said in the *Shiva Sūtras* (III, 22) that with the equalizing of *prāna* the spiritual aspirant sees equality everywhere: *prāna-samāchāre samadarshanam*. Then he becomes a perfect yogi, for his intellect abandons all sense of the limited "I" and realizes its oneness with the all-pervading cosmic intelligence. In this connection, the *Spanda Kārikās* (II, 5) says:

iti vā yasya samvittih kridātvenākhilam jagat,
sa pashyansatatam yukto jīvanmukto na samshayah.

He who knows and regards the entire world as a sport of
the Divine, being ever united with the Universal
Consciousness, is without doubt liberated even while alive.

A spiritual aspirant blessed by the Guru's grace becomes filled with joy upon recognizing this active world as nothing but the projection of the divine, cosmic Kundalini. If he follows the right path, such an aspirant can lead a normal worldly life; it is not necessary for him to leave his household. Through visions, his awakened Kundalini always protects him. She fulfills all his wishes and aspirations. Nothing remains to be obtained by him in whose heart this Shakti enters.

This Shakti is described by Parashiva Himself in the *Shiva Sūtras* (I, 13): *icchāshaktirumā kumārī*, "Icchashakti, the power of will, is the ever-young maiden called Uma." The *Shiva Sūtra Vimarshini* explains:

sā cha kumārī vishvasargasamhārakrīdaparā.

That young lady is ever engrossed in the sport of creation
and destruction of the universe.

The Shakti, the active aspect of the Supreme Lord, which brings about the creation, continued existence, and absorption of the universe, is the Supreme Shakti Uma, also described in the *Shiva Sūtra Vimarshini* as follows: *paraiva pārameshvarī svātantrya-*

rūpā, "She is absolute and of independent will." She creates an infinite number of worlds out of nothing. She is the same Shakti that is awakened in a disciple by the Guru's grace. Can any spiritual practices be difficult for those whose Kundalini is awakened by the Guru's grace? Even salvation is within their easy reach. Such favored ones practice the easiest of the easy means of discipline. The power of *gurukripā* always saves them from degradation. Indeed, Kundalini automatically fills their hearts with supreme bliss, as described in the *Tantrasāra: svātantryamānanda shaktiḥ.* When this bliss-showering Kundalini, which rises forth spontaneously without ever needing the help of any object or means, awakens in a spiritual aspirant, not only is he delighted, but he becomes the very embodiment of supreme bliss.

The Shakti alone knows Herself, and She alone is fully aware of Her own true nature, as distinctly expressed in the *Tantrasāra: āmarshātmakatā jñānashaktiḥ.* She is the power which, while holding and containing the entire cosmos, ever rests in blissful merriment and is full of consciousness and intelligence. Nothing is unattainable to those in whom this Shakti becomes active because, as described in the *Tantrasāra,* she is able to assume any form She likes: *sarvākārayogitvam kriyā-shaktiḥ.* The *Shiva Sūtras* (III, 30) say that this Shakti is capable of creating many worlds on Her own screen, without any outside material: *svashakti-prachayo'sya vishvam.*

As we have seen, Chiti, which is the same as Parameshwari Yogamaya Kundalini, ever flashes forth, manifesting the universe of infinite forms with absolute independence by Her own power. When, by the Guru's grace, this divine Shakti becomes active in the heart of spiritual aspirants, salvation loses all its meaning, because they themselves become one with Chiti. This should not be at all surprising since the entire universe is, in fact, Chiti. The *sādhaka, sādhanā,* Guru, mantra, *prāna,* and *kriyā* are all abounding in Chiti. Chiti is the five elements, namely, ether, air, fire, water, and earth. All animals are full of Chiti. Truly, in every aspect, Chiti alone is the cause and effect of the universe:

chitiḥ vishvam sādhayati,
chitimāsādya vishvam bhavati,
chityām vishvamīshvaraḥ karoti,
chiteḥ vishvam bhavati,
chiteḥ vikāro vishvam bhavati,
chitau vishvam sthitamiti.

Chiti creates the universe; the universe comes into existence with the help of Chiti; God creates the universe in
Chiti; the universe is created from Chiti; the universe is the
modification of Chiti; the universe is stationed in Chiti.

Therefore, in this world, which is permeated by Chiti, there is no
real impediment to becoming that Chiti by the grace of the Guru.

Final Attainment

All the Vedas say that "this Self is Brahman" (*ayamātmā
brahma*). If, therefore, the entire universe is nothing but the
Lord Himself, it is the absolute truth that one can experience
divine bliss, or Universal Consciousness, by following the path
shown by the Guru. This is precisely the gift and teaching of
Bhagawan Shri Nityananda. The *Shiva Sūtra Vimarshini* states:

gururvā pārameshvarī anugrāhikā shaktiḥ.

The Guru is the grace-bestowing power of the Supreme
Lord.

At the time of initiation, it is the Guru who, in the form of
Shakti, enters the disciple. Soon after this, the disciple's entire
personality is transformed. From the *mūlādhāra chakra* at the
base of the spinal column to the *sahasrāra* in the crown of the
head, the Shakti performs innumerable strange activities; but
She resides in the heart of the disciple, so that he is always aware
of Her work and activities.

While in meditation, aspirants sometimes perceive funeral
pyres burning and everything around them in flames. Some

aspirants, out of fear, think of getting up from meditation and running away, but when they open their eyes, they see no fire. These and other similar experiences are real spiritual experiences and not mere illusions. Thereafter, the blazing fire changes into a saffron or golden light of divine beauty and remains visible almost until the attainment of perfection. In this light *sādhakas* often have visions of saints and sages, and some even receive divine mantras or herbs from Siddhas. Such mantras can bring about spiritual awakening in anyone, and such medicinal herbs can cure incurable diseases. Not all aspirants are favored with such divine gifts, but one who is so blessed no doubt becomes a great benefactor of humanity.

The aspirant next begins to hear different kinds of divine music. As he continues to listen to it intently, he develops the power of effortless concentration and becomes absorbed in the music itself. When he merges into the divine sound (*nāda*) and reaches a state of thoughtlessness, he experiences great joy, bliss, and peace. Through the constant linking of the mind to the divine sound, the aspirant reaches a stage at which he becomes free from all feelings of separateness, such as mine and yours, one and many. Then, having transcended the three ordinary states of waking, dream, and deep sleep, he remains in the fourth state of *turīya*, the transcendental state, where he becomes fully youthful and enjoys the extraordinary bliss and profound tranquility called *turiyānanda.* The *Shiva Sūtras* (I, 7) say:

> *jāgratsvapnasushuptabhede turyābhogasambhavaḥ.*

> Apparently being in one of the three states of waking, dreaming, or deep sleep, he ever abides in the *turīya* state.

This is the fruit of yoga attainable by *gurukripā.*

This yoga is also known as Siddha Yoga because it is accomplished only through a Siddha (a perfect yogi). Without the grace of a Siddha, it is very difficult to reach the superconscious state, even through the practice of yoga. This path is also known as Maha Yoga, the great yoga, because the essence of all yogas is included in it. Therefore, this approach to the Ultimate is called Siddha Yoga, Maha Yoga, Purna Yoga, Parashiva Yoga, or *gurukripā*.

By the Guru's grace, the unrivaled One, who is all-blissful, is revealed. This direct comprehension and immediate experience are amazing to the yogi and are spoken of in the *Shiva Sūtras* (I,12): *vismayo yogabhūmikāh*, "The successive stages of yoga are full of wonders."

At the completion of this yoga, at its ultimate fulfillment, the yogi becomes equal to Shiva, as stated in the *Shiva Sūtras* (III, 25): *shivatulyo jāyate*, "He becomes like Shiva." Just as a worm is transformed into a wasp by the contact of a wasp, or as water when poured into milk becomes milk, so also, by the touch or grace of the Guru and by the union of Shiva and Shakti in the *sahasrāra, jīva* — the soul with limited consciousness — becomes Shiva — the omniscient, omnipotent Absolute Being. That perfected yogi transcends family, caste, creed, race, and even the consciousness of his own body. Instead, the awareness of being one with Shiva (*Shivo'ham*) starts repeating itself in his heart.

After being initiated by the Guru, an earnest disciple, on continuing his spiritual practices regularly for a period of three, six, nine, or twelve years (the period depending on the disciple's caliber, purity of heart, intensity of practice, and spiritual development), is able to experience divinity within his own Self. Thus, he becomes Self-realized. The Mahashakti Kundalini, always residing in the heart of a yogi, gives him many wonderful experiences and molds him according to Her will. On one yogi She bestows poetic genius, and to another She gives erudition and wisdom. She may bathe a third in the ecstatic stream of divine love. All people in close association with such blessed yogis enjoy peace and happiness. Even nature is enamored of them for, wherever they stay, the trees and creepers grow luxuriantly, orchards bear fruit in plenty, flower gardens blossom in marvelous beauty, and fields yield the best of harvests. The surrounding groves and woodlands always remain green and are as refreshing and charming as celestial gardens. Wherever

Parashiva's Shakti, which manifests and expands the universe, is active, the trees and the foliage, fruits, and flowers bloom in abundance very naturally. It is true that the entire atmosphere around such yogis vibrates with joy, abounds with love, and is pervaded by their Shakti. Whoever goes there with love, devotion, and faith experiences the divine influence and radiation of the Shakti and feels peaceful within. All these wonders are due to the munificence of Maha Yoga.

After entering the *sushumnā*, the Mahashakti Kundalini reveals Her supernatural qualities, such as joy, strength, peace, and bliss, to the aspirant. Then he carries out his spiritual exercises with enthusiasm. Inspired by the ever-new and mysterious experiences of the Kundalini, he practices yoga regularly and punctually. Soon he feels the spontaneous rising of divine love within his heart. Just as an addict cannot give up his habit and is restless until he secures his daily dose of intoxicant, a student of Siddha Yoga cannot be calm and restful without his daily practice of spiritual discipline. As the seeker follows this regular practice, the Kundalini, which is seated in the *mūlādhāra*, gradually travels upward, piercing the *chakras* on Her way, until She reaches the *sahasrāra*, the thousand-petaled lotus in the crown of the head. Here, in the last phase of Her active form, she unites with Her Lord Shiva and becomes one with Him. When the Kundalini Shakti is thus pacified by uniting with Shiva in the *sahasrāra*, She becomes static. One who has completed the full course of yoga *sādhanā* is a perfect yogi. When, in this way, the Kundalini Shakti is thoroughly stilled in the *sahasrāra*, pure knowledge arises. The *Shiva Sūtras* (I, 21) state that with the dawning of pure knowledge one attains the perfection of the Supreme Lord: *shuddhavidyodayāchchakreshatva-siddhiḥ*. Thereafter, the yogi forgets his spiritual striving and remains ever absorbed in the supreme state. When he was under the veil of ignorance, he felt miserable, poor, imperfect, attached, and powerless; but after the awakening of the divine Shakti, he realizes that he is perfect, accomplished, nonattached, powerful, filled with love, and of divine nature. In the joy of his attainment, he utters, "I am bliss" (*ānando'ham*). Drinking a fresh cup of joy every day, he remains in a state of deep intoxication. Now he no longer suffers from the dual malady of birth and death, for they dare not appear before him.

Those whose divine Kundalini Shakti is awakened naturally become fully drunk by sipping from the spontaneous fountain of bliss within. Just as a drop of water that has fallen into the ocean sees water on all sides and, merging with it, acquires vast expanse and loses its separate existence, so also the yogi, in the spontaneity of his inner joy, visualizes himself as the Universal Spirit pervading the entire world and ultimately attains profound peace and repose in it. How one feels upon reaching this state is expressed in the following verse from the *Ishwara Pratyabhijñā* (I, 12):

> *sarvo mamāyam vibhava ityevam parijānataḥ;*
> *vishvātmano vikalpānām prasare' pi maheshatā.*

He who has realized that the entire universe is his Self, and knows that "all this glory of manifestation is mine," possesses the power of the supreme Lord even though different thoughts may play in his mind.

A yogi who perceives the great visible universe as a grand sport of his own Self or of the Supreme Spirit remains in the unchanging state of true knowledge, even though he may perceive differences. He sees the unfolding of Parashiva being manifested in all entities. He perceives Shiva in front and behind, above and below, and on all sides. He knows nothing except Shiva. He himself becomes Shiva. To him:

> *shivo dātā shivo bhoktā shivam sarvam idam jagat;*
> *shivo yajati yajñashcha yaḥ shivam so' ham eva hi.*

Shiva is the giver and Shiva is the enjoyer. Shiva is this entire universe. Shiva is the sacrificer and the sacrifice. "I am that Shiva."

CHAPTER TWO

THE NATURE OF GOD

God, the Supreme Being, the One without a second, is known by more than one name, and there are many paths and forms of *sādhanā* to reach Him. God is infinite and so are His names. Yogis call Him *Om*; *jñānis* call Him *So'ham* ("I am That"); some say He is *prajñā* (pure wisdom); some say He is *chaitanya* (Consciousness); and so on. One does not need a term to name the Nameless, but all these different names refer to the same entity called God. He is the Supreme Reality that the Upanishads call Brahman. Brahman can never be defined or described. It has no attributes but is of the nature of *sat, chit*, and *ānanda* (existence, consciousness, and bliss).

Different creeds and sects put forth various arguments and use every imaginable kind of logic to establish their own concept of God. Let anyone say anything; nevertheless, it is absolutely true that God does exist and that He is *sacchidānanda*.

All dogmatic preachers of religion have conceived of, described, and presented that *sacchidānanda* in a form which suits their own belief or conception. Some seek Him in the form of Lord Vishnu, love incarnate; others call Him Sadashiva, the embodiment of peace; some think of Him as a void, beyond the reach of the mind; and others describe Him as the supremely blissful Brahman. In fact, everyone's concept of God conforms to his own attainment, and therefore these views should be regarded as correct, but partial. However, *sacchidānanda* stands out as the truest and the closest description of the Godhead, which is an incomprehensible and indescribable Beyond.

There are also various arguments for and against the form and the formless nature of God. But the nature of the incomprehensible Supreme Lord does not need proof by arguments. Being all-powerful, it is certainly not difficult for the Formless to assume form for some specific purpose. If this attributeless, formless God can create the world with its numerous hills and dales, rivers and seas by His own greatness, it should not be at all difficult for Him to assume the physical forms that have come to be known as Rama, Krishna, Buddha, Christ, Mohammed, and so on. Thus, it is easy for the Unmanifest to become manifest in any form.

It is unnecessary to argue whether God has any attributes. Each devotee can, and should, worship Him according to his own approach, feeling, and sentiment. The amount of divine happiness derived by a devotee depends entirely on the intensity of his own feelings. Pure sentiment always brings high rewards. Some years ago in Maharashtra, there lived a saintly woman called Bahinabai. She was a Self-realized soul who worshiped Truth and saw everything in its proper perspective. In one of her poems she wrote, "Intense devotion begets the desired fruits and ultimately leads to salvation." The words of the Vedas, that even fire can be kindled by intensity of will, devotion, and faith, are true. Bhagawan Nityananda used to say that a devotee can perceive God in his own heart by pure devotion and faith.

God is kind, compassionate, and also generous in bestowing His grace. In order to realize that merciful One, a seeker must follow any one of the spiritual paths and follow the disciplines prescribed therein with an earnest heart. But at the same time, we must remember that it is not fair to consider all other paths and disciplines inferior to our own. Bigotry cannot please God, because He is never captivated by any ritual or any particular method of *sādhanā*. It is only out of compassion that He reveals Himself to devotees when He is pleased by their selfless love. One should go straight ahead on one's own path of *sādhanā*.

One who wastes his time in finding fault with or abusing other paths is indeed a stupid and unfortunate creature. Such an ignorant person is not entitled to have the vision of God. He invites and causes not only his own decline, but probably that of others. Genuine aspirants should beware of such pitfalls. God is one for all.

Bhagawan Nityananda used to say that it is the same power that has manifested itself as Rama or Rahim, Keshav or Karim, and again it is the same power that has manifested itself as Christ, Allah, Madhava, or Mahadeva. The Puranas, the Koran, and the Bible all speak of Him alone. The ultimate goal implied in the teachings of all books of religion is the same. Only those who have faulty conceptions and whose *tapasyā* (practice of spiritual austerities) is not pure and perfect think in terms of superior and inferior and create confusion. In fact, for all beings the earth is one and the sky is one, and similarly the air they breathe, the water they drink, and the food they eat is the same. Even the sustaining life-force and the all-pervading *chaitanya* are the same. The nature of joy that is felt in the heart is also one for all living beings. Where, then, lies the difference? Can a person who sees and preaches distinctions be considered a religious being?

By its very nature, the Godhead is supremely blissful. It is full of love and sees no differences whatsoever. To commit the crime of making the distinctions of mine and yours, superior and inferior, is not the way to worship God. On the contrary, it is love of God that develops complete peace, everlasting peace, and nothing but peace. A person turns to religion so he can have true inner peace. The peace that the ancient sages attained within their innermost selves is attainable not only by Hindus, but equally by the followers of the Bible and the Koran. This is because the peace that spontaneously rises in the heart is essentially the same for all. He who resides in everyone's heart is full of peace, bliss, love, and wisdom and is effulgent and omnipresent. He is that most subtle Absolute Truth, the adorable God of all beings, and That alone is *sacchidānanda*, or the Godhead.

SACCHIDANANDA

Let us now try to understand the meaning of the word *sacchidānanda*, which is the true nature of God as realized by the sages, the knowers of Truth.

The term *sat* indicates that which exists in equal proportion in all beings, at all times, and in all places. The *ātman* pervades everything in full measure and is the support of all. Every visible object therefore rests in the *sat* aspect of God. Nothing exists without a support. Houses, factories, temples, mosques, and all other buildings are supported by the earth. Gold is the basis for all golden ornaments. Cotton thread forms the warp and woof of different types of cotton cloth. In the same way, God is the basic essence of which the entire universe is made. In other words, God is the fundamental fiber from which the entire pattern of the universe springs. That is why God is *sat*, real existence, and is the moving force behind the process of creation, sustenance, and dissolution of the universe. He is everything. He is Reality itself, and therefore Truth is His very nature. A seeker of Truth therefore attains God.

The second aspect of God is *chit*, which means cosmic intelligence or knowledge. *Chit* is also called Chiti, the Universal Consciousness. Chiti is that which at all times and in all places manifests or discloses everything as it is. Like the candlelight that makes things visible in the dark, *chit* reveals whether or not an object exists. *Chit*, which imparts life or consciousness to all and shines forth through all objects, is Chiti itself. The vision of the eyes, the hearing of the ears, and the power of speech are all the functions of that very *ātman*, which is Consciousness. This power is known as Chiti because it is the light of the sun and the moon and the effulgence of fire. It is the light of all lights in the universe. This very Chiti shines in the form of a divine, lustrous flame in everyone's heart, forehead, and *sahasrāra*. Fortunate *sādhakas* see this light during meditation by the grace of the Guru. However, even when it becomes visible, it is not different from the Absolute Brahman, which has no form or attributes.

This Chiti is the sovereign power governing all life, and hence it cannot be the exclusive possession of any particular sect or creed. Just as, according to Vedanta, this world is an imagination of the mind superimposed on the *ātman*, so are all the different faiths of the world creations of the mind, yet not separate from Chiti. Only pure Chiti (cleansed of all impurities and ignorance) can enter or be admitted into the greater Universal Chiti. Just as a river loses its name and identity when it merges into the vast ocean, so is an individual admitted into the realm of infinite wisdom when all his man-made cults and creeds cease to exist. In that supreme wisdom, all imaginary beliefs and faiths melt away and the vanity of their followers also evaporates. To Chiti, the entire world is its own manifestation. In its realm there is no inequality; only for people who have not been fortunate enough to receive the grace of the Guru does inequality exist. How could the Chidrupa Paramatman (Lord of wisdom) ever distinguish between Rama and Rahim, or Christ and Krishna, when such differences do not exist for those who have realized the Truth by His grace? It is Chiti that pervades the entire conscious manifestation. One who realizes Chiti perceives the entire world and all the different religions as existing in that Chiti, and nothing else. To say that the entire world is the manifestation of *chidātman*, the all-knowing Self, is the same as saying that the entire world is Chiti itself.

The third aspect of God is *ānanda*, that is, joy or bliss. The *Taittirīya Upanishad* (III,6) says that Brahman is bliss. All things are born out of bliss, are maintained by bliss, and ultimately merge into bliss. The Vedas and other scriptures, the seers, the sages, and all the enlightened ones unanimously affirm that bliss itself is the Supreme Lord. In fact, every activity in our life is motivated either to express joy or to acquire joy. A child is born out of happiness. We develop and sustain mutual relations with a view to becoming happy. Our striving for progress is also meant to bring more happiness. We undertake all our activities and fulfill all our duties not to create more sects and dogmas, more paths and divisions, but rather to experience more bliss and happiness in life. Why does a human being seek joy in everything? It is because the very nature of the Self is *ānanda*, or bliss.

Just as *sat* pervades everywhere, so also *chit* fills everything in full measure. *Sat* is *chit*, and *chit* is *ānanda*. Therefore, *ānanda* too fills everything fully. All our mutual relations are based on love. Is not a mother's love for her child pure and selfless? Do we not find older people loving younger ones just for the sake of love? The sweet smile of a child playing merrily in the lap of its mother, a husband's love for his wife or the unreserved sacrifice of a wife for the love of her husband, the willingness of a disciple to surrender everything unconditionally at the feet of his Guru, and the grace with which the Guru bestows on the disciple the gift of his own inner bliss, which makes him dance in ecstasy and awakens him from the evil dream of imaginary grief —all these support the view that the soul, which is born out of bliss, is bliss itself.

Tender shoots of corn grow merrily into ears of corn; new foliage blooms and beautiful flowers blossom; the sun and moon rise and set regularly, playing in their own delight; the galaxies of stars and constellations twinkle and illuminate the sky; the wind dances in all directions, drunk with its own joy, blowing its own music into every home; and the rippling waters of rivers and rivulets flow continuously, singing the name of the Lord; a person in distress is consoled by the kind words of a happy soul; the holy waters of the Ganges gladly wash away all impurities and sins, and bring peace and piety; Mother Earth cheerfully bears the burden of the entire world and offers fresh, ever-new harvests of infinite variety out of the fullness of her deep love; the cuckoo sings sweet melodies; and the *chataka* bird gives out its cries of love. Why are they all so happy? It is because they are born out of Brahman, whose very nature is joy and bliss. Bliss is the Supreme Lord. And all the Upanishads declare that the Supreme Lord is *sacchidānanda*.

JIVATMAN

Vedanta philosophy declares that *jīva*, the individual, and Brahman, the Absolute, are one. It is true that the *jīvātman* (individual soul) is the same as Paramatman (the Supreme Self). The Supreme Self projects itself in the form of individual selves and again merges into its original Self. The Lord declares in the *Bhagavad Gītā* (XV,7) that all individual selves are part of the Lord's own eternal Spirit, *mamaivāmsho jīvaloke jīvabhūtaḥ sanātanaḥ,* for none other than the Lord can become a *jīvātman.* The *Taittirīya Upanishad* (II,6) says, *tat srushtvā tadevānuprāvishat,* "Having created it, He Himself entered into it." Having created the physical bodies of all creatures, Paramatman Himself entered into them to make them alive and active. Is it the fleshy human mechanism that can make the eyes see or the tongue speak, that gives the power of hearing to the ears or the power of smell to the nose? Does the flesh have the power to see anything? No. It is Consciousness—the soul—residing and vibrating in the inner sanctum of the human temple that makes the senses function. The *ātman* is absolutely pure, perfect, and changeless. It is so pure that none of the good or bad qualities of the physical body can affect it.

The *ātman* exists in infinite physical bodies and yet remains untouched by them. It may seem to be tainted by the impurities of the mind, but if one follows yoga practices as instructed by the Guru, the mind and senses are purified of all thoughts and desires. Then the *antahkarana* (inner being) becomes extremely subtle. Such a perfectly pure *antahkarana* is by all means ready to receive and experience divine bliss. It is indeed possible, at that stage, to attain realization of the ever-pure inner Self.

Jīvātman, by its very nature, is pure, divine luster. Saint Kabir said:

saba ghata sāī rame hai,
sūnī seja nā koī.

God dwells in everybody; not even one form is left out.

In the *Bhagavad Gītā* (XVIII, 61), the Lord tells Arjuna that God
dwells in the heart of every being: *īshvaraḥ sarvabhūtānām hrud-
deshe'rjuna tishthati.* Bhagawan Shri Nityananda used to tell the
same thing to *sādhakas*: "God is within you. Why are you searching for Him in jungles? Why all these unnecessary wanderings?"
In the *Sadāchar*, Shankaracharya says:

> *deho devālayaḥ prokto,*
> *dehī devo niranjanaḥ.*

> The body is spoken of as the temple, and the indwelling
> soul as the immaculate God.

In other words, the human body is a holy temple, and the *jīvātman* that dwells within is none other than Paramatman. This
identity of *jīvātman* and Paramatman is realized when the state
of *So'ham* ("I am That") is actually experienced after complete
purification of the mind. But this realization becomes possible
only when the Sadguru bestows his grace upon the disciple. As
the wise say, the indwelling soul is concealed by a thin but tough
veil of ignorance, which does not allow us to know the purity
and perfection of that soul. This ignorance is burned up in the
fire of yoga; which is kindled by the grace of the Guru through
shaktipāt. The individual soul then truly realizes
its identity with the Supreme Self and is inspired to repeat
Shivo'ham ("I am Shiva"), the greatest of all mantras.

This *jīvātman* clings to its limited individuality only so long
as it does not realize its true Self. This is an imaginary bondage that makes the soul think of itself as imperfect. The
Pratyabhijñāhridayam says:

> *ayam shaktidaridhraḥ samsārī uchyate.*

> One who has become poor in Shakti is called a transmigra-
> tory being.

In other words, a soul that has no knowledge of the true nature
of the Self and has remained unenlightened because of its fail-
ure to earn the grace of the Guru, considering itself to be only a

flesh-and-blood body, is unhappy and aware of duality because of its ignorance. But as the *Pratyabhijñāhridayam* further says:

svashaktivikāse tu shiva eva.

With the unfolding of his inherent Shakti, however, one is Lord Shiva Himself.

In other words, one who has searched within, who has studied Vedanta philosophy well, who has practiced yoga and meditation, whose ego is completely annihilated, and who is devout, pious, and unattached, sees God within himself by the grace of the Guru. When the disciple's latent Shakti unfolds itself fully by the Guru's blessings, the feeling of "I am *jīva*" (*jivo' ham*) vanishes, and the knowledge that "I am Shiva" (*Shivo' ham*) dawns. That blessed soul then permanently lives in the awareness of "I am Shiva." This is like an ordinary soldier becoming a king because of some past merit, never again to revert to his former position.

Lord Krishna says in the *Bhagavad Gītā* (IV, 37):

jñānāgniḥ sarvakarmāni bhasmasātkurute tathā.

The fire of knowledge burns all karmas to ashes.

When, through the grace of the Guru, the divine spark of knowledge burns up the veil of ignorance, the disciple has a direct glimpse of the true nature of his Self and is enraptured by the pure bliss of the Self (*ātmānanda*). This is fulfillment or beatitude, which is the same as enlightenment or Self-realization.

CHAPTER THREE

GURU AND DISCIPLE

The many different powers we see in this world are nothing but different manifestations of God. Among these, the Guru is the most glorious manifestation of that Supreme Self, and so the Guru is known as the very embodiment of Supreme Reality: *guruḥ sākshātparābrahma.* The greatness of the Guru is described in the *Shiva Sūtra Vimarshini:*

gururvā pārameshvarī anugrāhikā shaktiḥ.

The Guru is the grace-bestowing power of the Supreme Lord.

In India all those who have been known for their achievements became great only by their Guru's blessings. The greatness and glory of Kabir Sahib, Jnaneshwar Maharaj, and Shri Eknath Maharaj originated from the gift of the blessings of their Guru. The Guru is therefore called *kalpavriksha,* the celestial tree, which fulfills every desire. The fortunate one who is blessed by the Guru's grace transcends human limitations and attains divinity.

As we understand the nature of the Guru more and more, we come to realize that the Guru is the embodiment of all gods, the essence of all that is holy, and the power that awards the fruit of all good deeds. One who seeks refuge at the feet of the Guru creates a heaven for himself and lives happily.

A real Guru is one who is well versed in the holy scriptures,

34

has identified himself completely with the Supreme Self, is capable of dispelling every doubt from a disciple's mind by convincing him thoroughly of the Truth, and can give the direct experience of Self-realization to a worthy disciple. The Guru's greatness, therefore, is infinite.

One who guides aspirants on the divine path is called a Guru. Teachers are held in high respect not only in India but in countries all over the world. The greatness of one who can transmit the divine power of his own soul to a disciple is beyond words. The divine gifts of the Guru are incalculable.

The Guru's consciousness remains permanently one with that of the Universal Self. That is why the Guru is everywhere, even when he appears to be present at one place. He is looked upon as a manifestation of Supreme Reality because he is the knower of the highest Truth and is firmly established in it, having achieved the direct experience of the Divine.

The Guru is not bound by the distinctions of any particular class or order of life. He is far beyond the formalities of religious or worldly duties since he has become one with the Supreme Self, which is the source of all purity. Body-consciousness cannot remain alive after the final realization. Such an individual remains steady in the experience that everything abides in him because he is the embodiment of pure Consciousness, the indivisible Brahman.

Intense devotion for and service to such a Sadguru indeed results in the divine attainment, which is the highest reward of all spiritual endeavor.

> *sacchidbrahma guruḥ sākshāt*
> *pūjyam sevyam aharnisham;*
> *rāmakrishnādidevānām*
> *sadguru brahma tārakam.*

The Guru, who is the visible form of *sat, chit,* and Brahman, should be worshiped and served day and night. Even Rama and Krishna received enlightenment through the Sadguru.

The Guru possesses superhuman powers, and that is why even divine beings like Lord Rama and Lord Krishna showed that one can obtain Self-knowledge by surrender at the feet of the Guru. We may be inclined to treat this as mythological legend, but we should remember that in the recent past a young, educated atheist named Narendra was completely convinced of the divine power of the Guru by accepting Shri Ramakrishna Paramahamsa as his Guru, and obtaining his grace through diligent service. He became famous as Swami Vivekananda, who is held in high esteem by the entire world.

In fact, the Guru is the soul of everything. The world is the manifestation of the Guru, and the Guru is the world in essence. The entire world, with all its movable and immovable contents, is the Guru. The Universal Consciousness, which is the cause and the basis of all creation, is itself the Guru. That same Guru is the power of action in the animate world. He is also the power of knowledge in all living beings, and it is he who works as the supreme willpower.

After awakening the spiritual force in a disciple, the Guru becomes its protector and controller. It is the Guru who manifests himself in the form of divine power in the heart of deserving disciples. It is the Guru who shines forth in and through the disciple, just as it is the father who is born in the son.

There are many types of gurus, but only one who is well versed in all scriptures, and who is capable of making a disciple attain the highest bliss by destroying his limited individuality and making him experience his identity with the Supreme Self through *shaktipāt*, is worthy of the highest adoration.

The more profound our reverence and regard for the Guru, the deeper and firmer our spiritual progress becomes. A story from the *Chāndogya Upanishad* narrates how, under orders from the Guru, all the elements appeared in person and explained their secrets to a disciple called Satyakam Jabala, who diligently obeyed the Guru's instructions. Jabala was asked by his Guru to tend four hundred cows in the jungle and return only when they had multiplied to one thousand. Obeying his

Guru's command, Jabala took the cows to the jungle and looked after them with utmost care, while he himself subsisted on what the jungle could give him in the form of roots and fruits. He constantly remembered his Guru and performed his duty with an unwavering mind, even in the most trying circumstances. After some years, when the number of cows had finally increased to one thousand, Jabala prepared to return to his Guru. The very thought of meeting the Guru in person and having the holy *darshan* of his sacred feet made his heart overflow with joy. While he was on his way, the five elements of the universe, pleased at his single-minded devotion to the Guru, manifested themselves before him one by one and revealed the secret and essence of their working.

Even the worship of the Guru's clay image brings these results, as the story of Eklavya from the great epic, the *Mahābhārata* illustrates. Eklavya came from a backward tribal family, and so Dronacharya, the Guru of the royal princes, refused to teach him archery, thinking that it might be misused. Eklavya was, however, determined to learn the science and had unflinching faith in the power of the Guru. He therefore made a clay image of Dronacharya and started worshiping it. By constant meditation and repetition of the Guru's holy name, his entire being became one with the Guru. Through such deep contemplation, the Guru's power spontaneously shone in his heart and imparted full knowledge of the science of archery to him. He automatically learned all that Dronacharya knew. He even learned the great secrets that Dronacharya himself had not taught to anyone. If so much power could be invoked even in a clay image of the Guru, could anything be impossible to achieve by praying, serving, and worshiping the Guru himself, who is the living embodiment of Brahman, the Supreme Reality?

There is also the story of Giri, an illiterate *brahmin* boy who became highly proficient in Vedanta merely by his rare devotion to Shri Shankaracharya, whom he had accepted as his Guru. He was a simple and devoted soul who fully believed that service to the Guru was the source of all knowledge. He therefore devoted himself faithfully to the service of the Acharya. He never neglected his duties and was always quick to perform every possible service to the Guru. Whenever the Acharya taught Vedanta to his pupils, Giri would very humbly stand by and listen. One day the Acharya held the class as usual but would not start the lesson. When the pupils asked him if he was waiting for someone, the Acharya replied that he was waiting for Giri. The pupils laughed and said, "Gurudev! Giri has gone to the river to wash your clothes. You may begin the lessons. It doesn't matter whether Giri is present or not since he doesn't understand or grasp anything."

This callousness pained Shankaracharya. In order to emphasize the value of *gurubhakti* (devotion to the Guru) and remove the pupils' false pride in intelligence and book-learning, he taught them not to belittle an illiterate, but devout, *sādhaka*. By his mere wish, he transmitted his grace to Giri. Instantly, the boy was inspired to compose Sanskrit verses in praise of the Guru, and with the Guru's clothes in his hands, he returned and stood before Shankaracharya, reciting the verses with humility. All the pupils were surprised by this miraculous change in Giri and at once realized their mistake. Giri thus became an enlightened soul by the grace of the Guru and became well known as Totakacharya. This is the greatness and power of *gurubhakti*. Let us now look at the qualities of a true disciple and the nature of his devotion to the Guru.

A TRUE DISCIPLE

Discrimination (*viveka*) and nonattachment (*vairāgya*) are the two main qualifications of one who wishes to be a disciple.

The ancient seers described mundane existence as dry, insipid, deceptive, ephemeral, and filled with suffering. Even Lord Krishna says in the *Bhagavad Gītā* (IX, 33) that this world

is fleeting and full of unhappiness: *anityamasukham lokamimam.*
One poet sings:

aba to gāfil jāga re . . .
dekhate murajhāya jāya kyā karatā hai rāga re,
jāga re nara jāga re.
māyā-jāla bichhāyā hai, lambe isase bhāga re,
jāga re nara jāga re.

Wake up at least now, O careless one. Why waste your
love on a world that is transient? O man, wake up; oh,
wake up. Flee from this illusive net of *māyā.* O man, wake
up; oh, wake up.

A person's suffering starts from the moment he is conceived. After a long, miserable confinement in his mother's
womb, he is finally born as a helpless baby, entirely dependent
on others. As a youth he is plagued by all sorts of temptations
and greed, and as an adult he is burned in the fire of lust and
worldly desires. Finally, he reaches old age with all its infirmities,
ugliness, fears, and helplessness. Where is the pleasure then? The
truth is that an individual soul is born in this world to reap the
fruits of its many good and bad past deeds. It lives for a while,
dies, and is born again; thus, the cycle of birth and death goes on.
Where are all the great kings and mighty warriors who once
ruled this earth? Where have they all gone? The world we see is
transitory and ever changing. That alone is true and real which is
eternally free and changeless, not bound by the limits of time,
space, and causation. The *ātman* is true, pure, perfect, immortal,
tranquil, and beautiful. Anything other than the *ātman* is not
real, for it changes and perishes with the passage of time. From
time immemorial, there have been innumerable great beings.
Where are they now? Just as the past has not survived, so the
present order will also perish in the future. One who has this
understanding and can discriminate between the eternal and
the transient is fit for initiation on the divine path. Such a person has a genuine desire to realize the true nature of human

beings, God, and the world, as well as to know the significance of *yoga, bhakti,* and *jñāna.* Therefore, he honestly follows the path shown by the Guru and is indeed a blessed seeker.

A true disciple is one who merges his entire individuality into his Guru. Such a disciple himself becomes a Guru in course of time. In fact, a true devotee is one who has merged his identity with God; a perfect yogi is one who is always in communion with the inner Self; and, likewise, a true disciple is one whose soul is forever united with the Guru.

In the *Gītā* (XVIII, 73) Arjuna says to Lord Krishna, *karishye vachanam tava—* "I will do Thy bidding." We can therefore say that one who has complete faith in the Guru's words and lives in complete accord with his wishes is a true disciple. Jnaneshwar Maharaj says that the words of the Guru purify the mind: *guruvachani mana dhutale.* Such a disciple inherits a great spiritual legacy and in due time attains the position of Guru. An ideal disciple is studious, attentive, alert, practical, and dutiful and has complete faith in the Guru's teachings. A disciple perfect in *gurubhakti* breaks the bondage of worldly existence, cuts the tie of delusion, and burns the net of obstacles through the strength of his devotion, dispassion, and discrimination. He is not carried away by the river of illusions nor parched by the fire of sufferings and sorrow. He is afraid of no one, nor does he frighten anyone; he is neither a coward nor a tyrant.

The subject of discipleship is very difficult to understand, and its secrets are beyond the conception of most people. There is hardly anything to match the greatness of a *sādhaka* who qualifies for discipleship by purifying his mind thoroughly. There are many teachers in the world, but illustrious disciples, such as Jabala, Eklavya, Totakacharya, Gavba, and Vivekananda, are rare. Just as Eklavya, though born in a low caste, became a master archer by his single-minded devotion to his Guru Dronacharya, so also Gavba, an illiterate disciple of Eknath Maharaj of Paithan, completed the unfinished *Bhāvārtha Rāmāyana* of his Guru. Gavba was the son of a poor widow. He was very fond of sweets, particularly *pūran poli* (sweet flat breads), which his poor mother could not afford. One day, the mother lost all her patience and took the boy to Eknath Maharaj, whose fame had spread far and wide. Eknath Maharaj was moved by the mother's plight and asked the boy if he would stay with him if he got *pūran poli* every day. The boy agreed to stay. Because of his excessive love for *pūran poli*, he was nicknamed Puranpolya. He never learned anything and was considered foolish and crazy. He was, however, extremely devoted to Shri Eknath and willingly did all the work that was allotted to him. He worshiped Eknath. He meditated on Eknath. He worked for Eknath. For him, Eknath was everything that mattered. At this time, Eknath Maharaj was nearing his *mahā-samādhi* (a yogi's final, conscious exit from the body), and one of his great works, the *Bhāvārtha Rāmāyana*, was likely to remain incomplete if the saint passed away. All of the devotees were worried, but Shri Eknath allayed their fears, and also surprised them, by declaring that his work would be completed by the illiterate Gavba. He then placed his hand on Gavba's head and infused him with the very spirit of his own inspiration. This transformed Gavba into an inspired soul, and the verses he composed thereafter are not distinguishable from those composed earlier by Shri Eknath Maharaj himself. The grace of the Guru and the devotion of the disciple thus elevated the disciple to the position of the Guru.

The ancient sages expounded various means—such as austerity, penance, repetition of the divine name, charity, religious vows, fasting, pilgrimages, image worship, and meditation on the Formless—for acquiring fame and fortune and becoming pure and noble. They are, no doubt, true and rewarding. Even so, for a genuine *sādhaka*, a seeker of the highest Truth, Shishya Yoga—that is, accepting discipleship under a Sadguru and proceeding on the spiritual path according to his teachings, instructions, and guidance—is the best. Shishya Yoga, the path of discipleship, is great in every respect.

Today there are swamis, philosophers, and lecturers on religious subjects who openly refute the tradition of discipleship and, by so doing, automatically eliminate the sacred tradition of the Guru. Such people not only blindly follow the wrong path under some delusion, but also lead others into the wilderness. There are also book-learned scholars, so-called *jñānis* devoid of any direct experience of the Divine, people with hearts completely lacking in the warmth of devotion, and similar insipid types who pose as spiritual guides. There are some self-styled teachers as well who have neither learned the basic techniques of yoga, nor acquainted themselves with the direct inner experience of wisdom through any Guru, but who still assume the position of Guru and start guiding others. Can a person who has not accepted anyone's discipleship, who has not obtained any knowledge from a Guru, be the guide or the Guru of others? What can a pauper give in charity? How can an illiterate person teach, or a blind man lead? What is there to give if one has not received? Such people give discourses on philosophy, guide their listeners, and, strangely enough, simultaneously denounce the sacred tradition of the Guru. Could there be a greater paradox?

What is discipleship? Discipleship, the acceptance of a Guru, implies unconditional surrender at the feet of the Guru. The underlying idea is difficult to comprehend. To be a disciple is to belong to the Guru wholeheartedly through love, devotion, faith, meditation, understanding, and direct spiritual experiences. Just as a droplet of water becomes the ocean by merging with it, so also does the disciple become identical with the Guru within a short time by uniting himself with the Guru in his own heart through pure love and devotion.

The scriptures speak of two types of sons: one is known as *vīryajata*, and the other as *mantrajata*. A *vīryajata* son is born from the father's semen, while one who is initiated by a Guru through *shaktipāt* and mantra *dīkshā* is the Guru's *mantrajata* son. In fact, spiritually, the latter relationship is more real than the former. The Guru transmits into the disciple his lustrous *mantravīrya*, which is potent with the power of penance, yoga, and *jñāna*. The *mantravīrya* is the very essence of supreme knowledge, and it transforms the disciple into a wonderful new being, full of the burning fire of yoga. In other words, the Guru transforms the disciple into his own prototype; then the disciple becomes identical with the Guru.

How does a disciple attain oneness with the Guru? He becomes one with the Guru by subduing the ego and merging himself completely into the Guru through every thought, word, and deed. By constant contemplation of the idea that the Self is the Guru and the Guru is Parashiva, the supremely benevolent Godhead, the disciple attains perfect, indivisible union with him. Such a one is indeed a true disciple.

A disciple who surrenders totally, without holding anything back, becomes the very image of the Guru through constant reflection and unceasing meditation upon the Guru. This is like the transformation of a larva into a wasp by the larva's contact with the wasp. Such a disciple is indeed true and great.

Many people ask why all the disciples of the same Guru do not make uniform spiritual progress or turn out to be exactly the same. This is because of the difference in their standards and abilities. All are not equally worthy or virtuous, and therefore, even though several disciples may be initiated by the same Guru, in one the divine Shakti may develop and shine fully, in another it may show only partial development, while in a third it may not show any visible effects at all.

After having experienced the spiritual greatness of the Guru, a true disciple does not raise doubts about the Guru's way of life, behavior, dealings, or method of teaching. Such skepticism obstructs a disciple's march toward spiritual perfection and attainment of Guruhood. One who tries to find fault with Gurus and thinks that they, like other human beings, are governed by passions such as anger or hatred does not deserve to be called a disciple. Discipleship implies complete dedication to the Guru and thus getting in return everything that the Guru can give. One who gives in full gets back in full. If a disciple holds something back, he gets that much less in return from the Guru. If, by the will of God, a Guru is hallowed with glory, surrounded by wealth, honored by the world, or happens to possess mystical powers or estates or ashrams, any number of people will rush to become his disciples with intentions all too apparent. But these are only wealth worshipers and bargain hunters. They are not true disciples fit to take the Guru's place of honor.

A disciple must be devoted to the Guru. A disciple's devotion is nothing but his selfless love for the Guru. *Bhakti* means love, and *gurubhakti* implies harnessing one's mind, body, and soul entirely in the service of the Guru, implicit obedience to the Guru, continuous remembrance of the Guru, and selfless love for the Guru. These qualities combined make a true disciple. Such a one is blessed by the gods. To him, all mantras bear fruit and all *siddhis* (mystical powers) easily accrue. If such a disciple happens to be a householder, he can easily realize God in the very midst of his family life; he does not have to leave his home in search of God. If, on the other hand, he has already renounced the material world, he very easily attains the state of Self-realization, which is the fulfillment of all desires.

A true disciple continues to be a disciple and retains the spirit of diligent service to the Guru even after attaining the highest state of yoga—the state of Self-realization—when he becomes an adept in *shaktipāt*.

A river of bliss flows through this divine union of the Guru and the disciple, in which countless people bathe to be purified and become holy.

CHAPTER FOUR

THE NECTAR OF LOVE FOR THE GURU

Love is *bhakti*, and *bhakti* means love. The awakening of deep and boundless affection for one's beloved Guru is love of Self, or *bhakti* (devotion). Such devotion is of the highest order and does not depend on formalities such as yogic practices, worship, rituals, or study. When the mind is desireless, when worldly objects do not attract it, when the wish for heavenly happiness and even the desire for salvation vanish, and with full affection the mind is firmly established in the lotus feet of Shri Gurudev, that state of the highest, all-exclusive love is known as *bhakti*. Such *bhakti*, such supreme love, is ambrosial in its very essence. To love only Shri Gurudev with all the intensity of the heart is real *amrit* (nectar). This *amrit* is the sweetest of all. One who receives and drinks it becomes immortal. Worldly desire is death.

An unwavering *bhakta* (devotee) always longs for the ever-fresh and pure love of his Guru. No other desire remains in his heart. He longs only for Shri Gurudev. Such a *bhakta* will see the divine form of his Gurudev, hear the sweet name of his beloved Guru, and utter softly the name "Shri Gurudev." His worldly life of give and take is filled with his Guru. In short, his only longing is for the lotus feet of the Sadguru.

When such a rare longing arises by Shri Gurudev's grace, the devotee, taking full advantage of this state of blissfulness which even the sages crave, becomes free from the cycle of birth and death. His heart then becomes Gurudev's temple. The union between an ardent devotee and the beloved Guru is in itself immortality. This culmination is the height of *gurubhakti*.

A devotee who has drunk *guru-premāmrit* (the nectar of love for the beloved Guru) has truly reached perfection. The power of this perfect state is incomparable and beyond the miraculous *ashtasiddhis* (the eight supernatural powers). A true devotee does not want these *siddhis*. When the real, the perfect, the source-of-all is achieved, the mind does not run after inferior and incomplete *siddhis;* the devotee does not even wish for salvation. Having reached the region of complete bliss, he is thoroughly satiated. Such a state of fulfillment and supreme joy, which is not easily attained even by gods and Siddhas, is enjoyed by the devotee on the strength of his devotion to the Guru, his Master. His worldly desires are extinguished by this fulfillment. He realizes that prosperity, beauty, sweetness, love, power, fame, and even knowledge and renunciation, which people always crave, are worthless compared to the rare love of a delighted soul. If one collects all the objects of the three worlds, they will not give the happiness equal to the supreme bliss that even a drop from the ocean of *nityānanda* (eternal bliss) will give.

In gain or loss, praise or insult, the devotee always remains cheerful. If he can gain the Guru's love and grace, the devotee, who has devoted his all to the service of the Master, does not care even if some obstacle comes in his way to salvation. His only earnest desire is that his love for the Guru will always increase. Being pleased and attracted by this love and devotion, God Himself showers joy-giving *amrit* in the devotee's heart. What could be more valuable than that love? Such a blessed devotee then lives perpetually in a state of blissful intoxication.

All the doubts of a devotee who has attained the nectar of knowledge from Shri Guru melt away. Knowing that the world around him is the *līla* (sport) of his beloved Guru, he becomes free of illusions. He can go where he likes. His Gurudev appears to fill the entire world. Is there a place where Shri Gurudev does not exist? Which object is not pervaded by Shri Guru? Gurudev is the source of all animate beings as well as inanimate objects of this world. The devotee knows that the entire universe is one with Shri Guru. The basic support of the universe is the super-conscious soul of Shri Guru alone. That which the Vedas describe after endless search as "not this, not this," which is even beyond the primordial sound *Omkār*, which is the root of all forms, and in which this complete universe exists—that eternal, unknown, indestructible Principle is beloved Shri Gurudev. He is the root of all religions—self-existent, immutable, and the ruler of the universe.

Having come to know the all-pervasiveness of the Master, the devotee may stay anywhere and still devote himself to his Gurudev. He can sing the prayers of love and devotion that are inspired by his heart. Such a devotee considers time, place, past, present, here, and there to be inseparable from Shri Guru. Just as the air molds itself in any form and moves everywhere, this devotee, being enlightened with the knowledge of the Self, joyfully moves in all three worlds.

To see and realize Shri Gurudev in all living beings is real devotion. This love for all comes through Shri Guru's grace and makes the devotee almost mad with love. He goes on singing the praises of the Master day and night. He hears, speaks, sings, and thinks of Shri Guru alone. Often, he acts in a manner that seems senseless to those who do not understand his state of divine intoxication. He remains absorbed in a state of intoxication with Guru's love. His heart melts with extreme love and adoration for the Guru, and when this state reaches its peak, the ecstatic devotee may sometimes laugh heartily, cry, shout, sing loudly, or even dance. In this sublime state, he experiences oneness with Shri Guru. His mind and body become calm and peaceful.

Life then becomes joyful and worthwhile for such a devotee. He alone is an *ātmārām* (one who is absorbed in the Self). Because everything is merged into Shri Guru, no ideas of distinction or duality, love and hate, mine and yours, small and great remain in him. This is oneness in love, a state of absolute nonduality attained through love. When the devotee is thus established in oneness with Shri Guru, his separate existence disappears altogether. The secret of achieving this unique state of love is abandoning the desire for worldly objects. Not only does the longing for money, husband or wife, children, fame, and heaven vanish, but in this intoxicated state not even the desire for liberation survives. The devotion that asks or hopes for something in return is a sort of selfish bargain filled with ambition.

In the *Bhagavad Gītā* Lord Krishna says:

ye hi samsparshajā bhogā duhkhayonaya eva te;
ādyantavantaḥ kaunteya na teshu ramate budhaḥ.

O son of Kunti, the joys derived from sensual contacts are the source of misery; they have a beginning and an end. The wise person does not delight therein.

It is a fact that the pleasure derived through the senses is not real happiness. It brings only misery in its wake. One who has earned the sweet love of his Guru is really happy. One who fails to obtain this love is allured by the senses and becomes entangled in sensual pleasures. Just as a starving man gulps down mud or sand, or a deer oppressed by thirst mistakes a mirage for real water and runs after it only to meet death, those who do not realize the worth of Shri Guru's love and are deluded by sensual enjoyments, lust, and wealth meet poverty and misery in the false name of happiness. A wise person who has completely freed his body and mind from impure tendencies by the constant remembrance and repetition of Shri Gurudev's name becomes pure.* His thoughts of likes and dislikes are easily destroyed. Where is there room for duality in the devotee's heart when the supreme bliss of Absolute Reality resides in all its grandeur? By experiencing eternal joy within himself, the devotee attains a state of Self-absorption that removes his entire ego. When ego and pride thus disappear, the individual soul, merg-

---

* Here, "Shri Gurudev's name" refers to the mantra given by the Guru.

ing in the sweet love of the Guru, so closely embraces him that at that very moment, like the mingling of a wave with the ocean, the soul of the individual becomes united with that of his Guru to become indivisibly one. When one looks at air in the sky, it is difficult to determine which is air and which is sky. Likewise, when the devotee and the Guru become spiritually united, all distinctions and inequalities are destroyed and only the essence, *nityānanda*, remains as the devotee's true Self. Differences having come to an end, only an unbroken flow of supreme joy remains. The *gurubhakta* then looks like the embodiment of joy. Renunciation of all desires is easily attained through intense love.

There is a natural flow of love in the heart of every individual. This is because each soul, being a part of the Absolute Reality, naturally possesses its essential qualities of intense joy and supreme love. But the stream of love is contaminated by its contact with sense objects. Hence, that pure love turns into passions, which bring endless miseries. As a result of these impurities in the stream of love, one cannot perceive the divine light of the Supreme shining within oneself. In order to enjoy the delightful supreme love and divine light, it is essential to change the course of the mind, which runs after earthly pleasures, and make it introspective. The mind can be bent in any direction. Unless it completely leaves the muddy pool of sensual objects, it cannot enjoy a swim in the ocean of eternal bliss. It is impossible to sing a song and chew hard nuts at the same time. After tasting nectar, who would relish sense delights?

Prayer is the only thing that gives rise to love in one's heart. One experiences nectarlike love for Shri Guru by constant repetition of and meditation on his name. Thus, devotional prayer is both a means and an end in itself. For one who has earned love for Shri Gurudev, meditation naturally becomes a continuous phenomenon. Hence, whoever wants to achieve love for Shri Gurudev should repeat his name unceasingly. A person who desires liberation without earning it with prayer, devotion, meditation, and renunciation is committing a grave mistake. He is deceiving himself. He is like one who cuts his own feet with an axe. After many years of constant meditation on Shri Gurudev and by repetition of his name with all sincerity and respect, love and devotion will arise in one's heart. In other words, it is absolutely necessary to learn and master the means to this end.

A devotee or spiritual aspirant should always avoid evil association. Bad company slowly gives rise to low tendencies, bad habits, and evil instincts. Furthermore, it destroys all the ennobling qualities inherent in human beings, and then all calamities follow. By listening to the ill advice of her maid Manthara, Queen Kaikeyi, who was a very loving, affectionate, and noble lady, became the cause of extreme grief and sorrow to King Dasharatha and all the people of Ayodhya. As a result, she became a widow and lost all the love and respect of her dear son, Bharata. Association with the evil-minded Shakuni is considered the prime cause of the battle in the *Mahābhārata*, which brought about terrible ruin and destruction. Therefore, one who wants happiness should stay away from all vices and wickedness.

God, love, delight, supreme happiness, absolute joy, and eternal bliss are just different names for the one Supreme Reality and knowledge. It is impossible to define Brahman. Even the Vedas remain silent after describing it as "not this, not this." Similarly, one cannot describe the sweetness of love for Shri Guru. Even in worldly life, the inner joy one experiences on meeting one's beloved, or on receiving news of one's sweetheart, is beyond expression. That which one puts in words is only the outer form of love. Actually love is to be felt, experienced, tasted. One who is fully immersed in the ocean of love is unable to utter anything, like a dumb person who only smiles when he tastes a lump of sugar but cannot speak about its sweetness. This is because there is no language that can explain divine love. When the heart is filled with that supreme joy, all outer consciousness is lost and one becomes silent.

This love is without any qualifications or desires. It grows every moment and is finer than the finest form of experience. It is nothing but the blissful soul of the Lord Shri Guru residing in the secret alcove of one's heart. This love is the highest joy. Being immersed in such divine *rasa* (that which is most relishable) of supreme delight, the blessed devotee is unable to see anything but his beloved Gurudev pervading everywhere. His complete self experiences him. All the senses concentrate on him alone. Day and night the eyes see the entire universe filled with him only, the ears hear incessantly the sweet mantra *Guru Om*, the tongue relishes uninterruptedly that juicy nectar of Shri Guru's sweet name, and the mind enjoys the presence of the loving Guru everywhere.

Gurudev is sound in the ether. He alone is felt in the touch of the air. He is the light in fire, the sweetness of water, and the fragrance of the earth — he alone fills everything. He is seen in all beings in various forms. Everywhere the blessed devotee feels the same joy and nothing but joy. The entire universe is full of Gurudev Shri Nityananda, who is love — delightful and full of nectar. Everything is filled with joy, beauty, and sweetness. Devotee and God are sweet; the object and the subject are both lovable. You and I and all are blissful. All that is pervaded by delightful and lovable Lord Shri Guru is sweet. The lover of the Guru, having attained this state, remains absorbed in the nectar of divine love for all time; yet that state of love is indescribable. Love is the very essence of the innermost core of *bhakti*. Love is also an immensely valuable and cherished possession, and it is indeed the highest limit of joy and happiness. There is nothing beyond this, and that nothingness itself is Nityananda, eternal joy and bliss, who presently resides in the form of a statue in the Guru Mandir of Gurudev Siddha Peeth in Ganeshpuri. Even his statue radiates powerful vibrations of his all-encompassing love. Innumerable men and women, *yati* and *muni*, pious and sinful, young and old, happy and miserable still come to have *darshan* of his lifelike and powerful image. They consider themselves blessed, are satisfied, and leave feeling happy.

CHAPTER FIVE

JAPA YOGA

In this Kali Yuga (the "Dark Age"), *nāma japa*,* or repetition of the name of God, is a highly potent means of acquiring divine knowledge and success in any endeavor. The secret of *japa yoga* is very profound and difficult to explain. It has limitless powers, by means of which aspirants can attain the highest yogic state with ease, however difficult, unknown, or incomprehensible it may be. *Japa yoga* occupies an important place in the sphere of spiritual science. It has been practiced from time immemorial by all classes of society the world over, by all traditions, religions, and faiths such as Vedic, Smarta, Tantric, Jain, and Buddhist, each in their individual ways. The practice of *nāma japa* affords equal protection to all without distinction. It serves everyone—high or low, *bhakta* or *yogi, jñāni* or meditator, rich or poor, foolish or wise, poet or artist, physically disabled or morally fallen. *Namāsmarana*, remembrance of God's name, can be fruitfully pursued by spiritual aspirants in any condition. As a seeker progresses in his practice, his love for God increases day by day and he gradually earns the grace of the Lord. His faith deepens, and he develops greater enthusiasm and courage in his spiritual pursuit.

The practice of *japa* is indeed a divine, nectarlike experience of spiritual endeavor, perfect in itself. It is well said:

* Mantra, *japa, shabda,* and *namāsmarana* are all synonyms.

shukasanakādi siddha-muni-jogī,
nāmaprasāde brahmasukha-bhogī.

Shukadev, Sanak, and other enlightened sages and yogis tasted the bliss of Brahman, or Supreme Reality, through the name of God.

The significance of *nāma japa* can never be adequately described. Lord Krishna says in the *Bhagavad Gītā, yajñānām japayajño' smi,* "Of all the *yajñas,* I am the *japa yajña"* — showing the superiority of *japa* among all offerings of prayers and sacrifices. *Japa* is *maha yajña,* a great sacrificial prayer, and it is the form of the Lord Himself. *Nāma japa* is also known as *japa yoga* (union through *japa*) because by destroying the veil of separation which has disunited us from our real, divine, and blissful Self, it reunites us with Supreme Reality, or God; it lets us enter the realm of our blissful Self. In other words, it reunites the soul with that Brahman which is One without a second. This is also known as realization of the all-pervading Consciousness.

In Maharashtra there once lived a great saint, Namdev, who was a *prema yogi,* a yogi of love. He advocated the practice of *namāsmarana* with intense love. Namdev epitomized his teaching in this way:

nāmā mhane nāma,
chaitanya nija dhāma.

The name of God is the very abode of Consciousness.

Thus, *nāma japa* is at once a means and an end. That it is the best means to God-realization has been very eloquently emphasized by great men and women through the ages: Goraknath, Gopichand, and Bhartrihari — who were *hatha yogis;* Janaka, Sanaka, Markandeya, and Bhagiratha — *raja yogis;* Narada, Dhruva, Prahlada, and Shuka — *mantra yogis;* Vrishabhadeva, Jadabharata, and Ajagar — *laya yogis;* and Mira, Janabai, Draupadi, and Chaitanya Mahaprabhu — *prema yogis.* These great men and women of Truth, who were indeed selfless and impartial, highly acclaimed *japa yoga* as a straight, royal road for those seeking salvation. The path of yoga known as *surat yoga,* which was followed by saints and seers in the Middle Ages, is the same as *vak yoga,* that is, *japa yoga.*

The difficult exercises of *ashtānga yoga,* the intricate rituals of *yajña* (to accomplish which one has to master textual passages of Vedic prayers, etc.), the all-absorbing contemplation on the sublime thought "I am Brahman" of *jñāna yoga* (in which one must first attain purity and subtlety of the mind before one is fit to pursue the path), and the cultivation of all-exclusive, supreme devotion and love for God, a prime qualification of *bhakti yoga*—all these paths are learned only by strenuous effort and therefore are not easy for everyone to fulfill. But aspirants who practice continuous remembrance of the mantra given them by their Guru can, without great effort, reach the same spiritual consummation as in all these paths:

> *japata pavanasuta pāvana nāma;*
> *apane vasha karī rākheu rāma.*

> Repeating the holy Name, Hanuman won Rama's love for himself.

Japa yoga is the best means of achieving the ultimate fruit aspired to by followers of different spiritual disciplines. Shri Shankaracharya* said:

> *sakalapurushārthasādhanam sukhasampādyam*
> *alpaprayāsam analpaphalam.*

> Japa is the most effective way of achieving the four-fold aims of life. It can be practiced with ease, and it yields great results with the least effort.

He further stated:

> *himsādipurushāntaradravyāntara-*
> *deshakālādiniyamānapekshatvam.*

---

* Shri Shankaracharya wrote a commentary on the *Vishnu Sahasranam* that is worth studying. There is also a work in Marathi called the *Nāmachintāmani,* in two parts. These works deserve to be read by all practitioners of *japa yoga.*

Practice of *japa yoga* does not require one to do a sinful act like killing [of animals for sacrifice]. It does not require help from any person or spending any money; nor is it limited to a fixed place or time.

The grace of a Guru alone is enough to enable one to practice *japa yoga* with very little effort. It is well said in the *Mahābhārata:*

> *japastu sarvadharmebhyaḥ paramo dharma uchyate;*
> *ahimsayā cha bhūtānām japayajnaḥ pravartate.*

Japa is the highest of all religious practices because *japa yajña* can be fulfilled nonviolently, that is, without killing of animals for sacrifice.

The great law-giver Manu said that by practice of *japa* alone a person can achieve success in his spiritual endeavor and attain perfection. He may or may not practice any other discipline. Indeed, all *siddhis* (that is, the material gains, such as health, wealth, and happiness, and even perfection that one longs to achieve) are acquired through *japa yoga*. The scriptures on mantra, *jñāna*, *bhakti*, and *yoga*, as well as the science of astrology formulated by sages, are all valid. They are subtle and profound. Only our own power of comprehension, which has inherent limitations and varies in degree, leads some of us to doubt the validity of these scriptures.

The science of astrology tells us that the actions of previous births confront us in our present birth in the form of *prārabdha* (destiny), and we have to reap their fruit, sweet or bitter, during this lifetime. Astrology describes the influence of the twelve signs of the zodiac on one's life, as well as the relative positions of the planets in these signs, thus indicating one's good or bad fortune. The future is seen according to the strength of the twelve houses in the horoscope. For instance, those whose *dhana sthāna* (house of wealth) is not strong or pure lead a life of penury. Those whose *putra sthāna* (house of children) is weak either do not have a child born to them, or have a child who goes astray.

Similarly, those whose *jaya sthāna* (house of partnership) is not good either do not get married or, if they do, become unhappy with their spouse. All this is true. Thus, as long as each of the twelve houses in the horoscope is not pure, one will not derive the full benefits signified by each. Yet a *sādhaka* who practices *nāma japa* with faith, devotion, and love is bound to derive the full benefits of all houses of the horoscope. This is because as he progresses in his *japa*, each of the houses gradually undergoes complete purification. First, his *tanu sthāna* (house of physique) is purified and his body becomes healthy. Then comes the purification of *dhana sthāna*. A poor seeker comes to enjoy prosperity, and a rich one becomes virtuous. The *parākrama sthāna* (house of valor) then becomes pure. The seeker develops qualities of courage, fortitude, and willpower whereby he becomes devout, religious, and fearless. The purification of *vidyā sthāna* (house of learning) endows the seeker with scholarship and erudition. That is why, when the process of purification of all the *sthānas* in the horoscope is accomplished by means of *japa*, the *japa yogi* begins to enjoy inner peace, happiness, and material well-being, and experiences the supreme bliss of communion with God as well. *Nāma japa* is a veritable *kalpavriksha* (wish-fulfilling tree) or *kāmadhenu* (celestial cow) to those who lead a worldly life. It is no exaggeration to describe *nāma japa* as *paramachintāmani* (a gem that yields anything desired).

MANTRA
Its Meaning and Potency

According to the *Mantra Shāstra*, there are as many as seventy million mantras. Many of these, such as *Om Namo Narayanāya, Rām Rāmāya Namah, Klim Krishnāya Namah, Om Namah Shivāya, So' ham, Shivo' ham,* and the *Devi Navarnava* mantra, are said to lead one to the realization of Brahman.

Continuous remembrance of such a mantra is *japa.*

Repetition of a mantra received from a Siddha Guru (a perfect Master) eventually leads one not only to the vision of one's chosen deity or knowledge of Supreme God, but also to the much coveted Self-realization, and yields happiness and all kinds of rewards. In fact, the mantra is powerful enough to take one very close to God. It is even capable of transforming a human being into God. Every spiritual aspirant should remember this fact. The highest aim of mantra is Supreme Shiva, or the Self, which is pure Consciousness.

It has been truly said, *ādau bhagavān shabdarāshiḥ*, "In the beginning, God was in the form of word," which means that Parashiva, the Supreme Being, is of the form of sound. Sound is as pervasive as space. The *chidākāsha*, that is, the space of Consciousness in the heart, is the seat of God. The sound of *japa*, once it enters the *chidākāsha*, has the potency to impart the highest enlightenment. In the *Mahānirvāna Tantra* it is said:

> *mantrārtham mantrachaitanyam yo na jānāti sādhakaḥ,*
> *shatalaksham prajapto' pi tasya mantro na sidhyati.*

This means that a person who practices *japa* without understanding its meaning and potency will not derive the fruits thereof, even if he repeats the mantra ten million times. It is therefore necessary to understand the mantra fully:

> *pruthang mantraḥ pruthang mantrī*
> *na siddhayati kadāchana;*
> *jñānamulamidam sarvam*
> *anyathā naiva siddhayati.*

If a mantra is recited with the idea that the mantra and its reciter are different, it will never yield perfection. This is basic. Without this knowledge about mantra, one will never achieve the result.

One cannot complete the *sādhanā* of *japa yoga*, that is, one cannot attain the highest fruit of practicing *japa*, if one lacks proper understanding and believes that the mantra, its deity, and its reciter are separate entities. In reality:

mantrāḥ mananatrānarūpāḥ shivādabhinnasvarūpāḥ

This means that the mantra has the potency to protect one who contemplates it; it is not different from Shiva. It makes one who constantly reflects on it attain oneness with Lord Shiva. That is why mantra is considered a form of Shiva.

vāchyavāchakayorabhedopachārāt
mantro mantradevatā;
evam mantrimantradevatāsu
ārādhyārādhakabhāvena
pruthagdhīḥ siddhim naiti.

Worship is done with an understanding of the identity of the named and the word that expresses the name; the mantra is itself the deity of the mantra. However, the idea that the reciter of the mantra and the deity of the mantra are different, and a feeling of distinction between the worshiper and the worshiped, will not be fruitful.

No distinction should be made between the deity of the mantra and the mantra that is recited. *Japa* and the deity whose *japa* is practiced are one and identical. The means and the end to be achieved are not different. The mantra itself is the deity invoked by the mantra. The successful completion of the repetition of the mantra calls for an inner feeling or understanding that the mantra, its reciter, and the deity connoted by the mantra are one and the same. Even a partial feeling of distinction among these three will bring very meager results for a *japa yogi.*

One who has sought all the details about mantra and its practice from the Guru who has given the mantra will achieve immediate results in his endeavor to perfect *mantra japa.* A *mantra yogi* must know and understand the supremely blissful God in the form of sound:

mantrā varnātmakāḥ sarve,
sarve varnāḥ shivātmakāḥ.

All mantras are composed of syllables, and all syllables are the very soul of Lord Shiva.

All mantras are composed of letters, and all letters constitute mantras. They are thus Lord Shiva; that is, they are completely of the form of Lord Shiva. In fact, the real nature of mantra is Maheshwara, the great Lord. The Lord is mantra in another form. Lord Shiva said to Parvati, the mother of the universe, *mantro madrūpāḥ varānane,* "O beauteous one, mantra is My very form." When a seeker recognizes the mantra as the very form of Lord Shiva, it rises forth spontaneously in the *chidākāsha* and helps him to attain identity with Shiva. For this reason, mantra is identical with Maheshwara. Indeed, mantra, the name of God, is as perfect as God Himself.

The great *rishis,* realized souls with deep insight, said that when a person becomes thorough in *shabda brahma,* that is, in the practice of *mantra japa,* the knowledge of the highest Reality dawns on him. Thus, to attain the Supreme, which is beyond words, one has to make use of *shabda* (the Word, or mantra) and then go beyond the realm of words. It is also said in the scriptures that this universe came into being through the Word and is sustained by the power of the Word. If one wishes to go beyond creation, then the Word is the vehicle. Therefore, in *japa yoga,* one is advised to reach the Supreme Reality through the means of *shabda.*

In mundane life, too, we learn and understand everything and carry out all our dealings through words, that is, through speech. News and reports about what is happening in the world are all communicated to us through words. When a person expresses his feeling or experience through speech, it is his own Self that is being revealed through the spoken word. Hence, a word is the very person who speaks it. Similarly, the all-knowing mantra, which is the Guru's own Self, resides in his heart in a live form as *prāna* and *apāna.* Therefore, the mantra imparted to a disciple, even if small, carries with it great potentiality, like the seed of a banyan tree.* The mantra given by the Guru, although

* The mantra to be chosen for *japa* should not be very long, because it is difficult to harmonize the repetition of a long mantra with the breathing process.

seeming to be mere syllables, has the divine potency to awaken
the highest yoga in a disciple. It has the power to burn up completely a *sādhaka's* accumulated *karmas*. On entering a *sādhaka*,
the mantra is capable of transforming him, of making him worthy of attaining oneness with Shiva.

Great sages who were *mantradrishta* (seers of mantra) spoke
of two types of mantras: *jada*, or inert, and *chaitanya*, or alive.
That which is completely free in all respects and which infuses
life into everything is *chaitanya*. That which, by reason of its full
independence, infuses life into the sun, the moon, the stars, the
lightning, and the elements, which activates the mind, the intellect, and *prāna* (vital force) in their respective functions by ani-
mating them, and which, though itself changeless, through that
inaction activates the entire inner and outer world consisting of
both the animate and the inanimate is none other than the Lord
of the mantras, the Parashiva Paramatman, the highest aim of
that extremely pure and live mantra. Just as the mantra is
Parashiva, the lord of the mantra is Parashiva, and Shri Guru is
also Parashiva.

When the Guru has made his mantra divine and alive, it is
known as *chaitanya* mantra. This mantra is perfect, liberating, a
precious divine gift, as well as the giver of all types of powers.
Along with the mantra, the Guru's *ātmashakti*, the power of his
soul, enters a *sādhaka* who practices *japa* regularly. A *chaitanya*
mantra is obtained from a Siddha Guru, through his grace. By
continuous repetition of such a mantra, the *sādhaka's* own
ātmashakti is awakened. By the awakening of the inner Shakti,
known as Kundalini, all the *chakras* are pierced. After the piercing
of the *chakras*, all the impurities of the body are completely
removed. Then the flow of *prāna* and *apāna* is equalized, and the
sushumnā (the central *nādī*) becomes active. When the *sushumnā*
fully unfolds, the seeker becomes one with Lord Shiva. As a result
of the union of Shiva and Shakti in the *sahasrāra*, one who has
finally established himself in that ever-blissful Shiva is recognized
as a Siddha; such an attainment is called the state of Siddhahood.
The *Shiva Sūtras* say, *siddhaḥ svatantra bhāvaḥ*, "Such a one enjoys

perfect freedom." Just as seed begets seed, so does an aspirant who obtains a *chaitanya* mantra from a Siddha Guru reach the state of a Siddha at the completion of his spiritual practice. On attaining this state, he enjoys complete freedom; no vestige of dependence ever comes over him again. His mind, senses, mental and psychic tendencies, and intellect are now under his control and can no longer agitate him. The Adi Guru, or first preceptor, Parashiva, initially imparted His Chiti Shakti, which is full of wisdom and bestows the highest bliss, to His devoted disciple. That disciple in turn imparted it to his disciple, and he to his disciple, and so on. Thus, through the Guru-disciple tradition, which has come down to us from time immemorial, the creative power (*kriyā shakti*), the immanent aspect of the changeless and inactive Parashiva, continues to be active. This activity belongs to yoga. That is why a mantra should always be obtained from a Guru.

The Self, or *ātman*, of the Guru never changes in its perfection. Whoever merges with the Guru becomes one with his Self, and that Self does not become diminished, severed, warped, deteriorated, or even increased. Always remaining in the same changeless, irreversible state, the Guru transforms his disciples just as the philosophers' stone turns iron into gold. Like a magnet, he activates the divine Shakti lying inert in his disciples. And like the holy waters of the Ganges, he makes his disciples as pure as he is and thereby makes his disciples' disciples perfect like himself. Thus, one who is identical with Lord Shiva in every way, who has imparted to other spiritual aspirants the divine Shakti by which they can bring their disciples to perfection, and who is thoroughly capable of giving the divine authority for *gurupad* (Mastership) to others, is alone Shri Guru. He is the transmitter of *mantravīrya* (essence of mantra) to his disciples. There is not the slightest difference between the Guru and Lord Shiva:

> *yo guruḥ sa shivaḥ prokto*
> *yaḥ shivaḥ sa guruḥ smritaḥ;*
> *ubhayorantaram nāsti*
> *gurorapi shivasya cha.*

This means that a worthy disciple, who by obtaining the divine
grace of the Master has become the Guru, is Shiva. Indeed, Shiva
becomes the Guru, and then no difference between the two
exists. The Guru is none other than the manifested form of
Lord Shiva: *sa gururmatsamaḥ prokto mantravīryaprakāshakaḥ*.
Here Shiva Himself says that the Guru who radiates the potency of mantra is like Shiva. Truly speaking, he is Shri Guru who
always remains the same at all times, in all places, and in all
things and who is all-pervading. According to the maxim *shivo
bhūtvā shivam yajet*, one who first thinks himself to be Shiva,
then worships Shiva, and ultimately becomes Parashiva, is the
Guru. The entire universe belongs to him because all animate
and inanimate things of the world are created, maintained, and
dissolved by him. Thus, although apparently inactive, he is
active. He, being the Guru, is the benevolent God of his disciples. Just as the boundless ocean makes all the streams of water
that flow to it like itself, in the same way the Guru who has
transmitted the essence of mantra, which is his own blissful
Self, into the disciple's heart and transformed him into his own
likeness is indeed Shri Guru, the knower of the potency of the
divine mantra. He is the destroyer of the worldly bondage of his
disciples. The Guru takes a human form to bestow the highest
good on devotees. By entering his disciples in the form of the
mantra, the Guru makes his life identical with the mantra. Just
as a caterpillar is transformed into a butterfly, so does a *sādhaka*
who has received the Siddha mantra attain perfection and
become like Lord Shiva.

> *tadākramya balam mantrāḥ sarvajnaḥ balashālinaḥ;*
> *pravartante'dhikārāya karanānīva dehinām.*

Thus it is said in the *Spānda Karikās* by Vasuguptacharya that
mantra contains all the powers such as omniscience. This power
of mantra starts the process of yoga in a *sādhaka* and gives him
all the *siddhis*; thus, mantra is the begetter of *kriyā yoga*. Both the
Guru and his mantra are the forms of Shiva. If a *sādhaka*
performs *mantra japa* while identifying himself with the Guru

who has imparted the mantra, the mantra itself, and the great Lord Shiva, then the mantra instantly activates inner yogic processes and very soon he becomes like Lord Shiva.

JAPA IN THE FOUR BODIES

Without true knowledge there is no liberation from the cycle of birth and death. An ancient *rishi* said, *jñānāt tu paramā gatih*, "Through knowledge, you attain the final beatitude." And again, the Lord says in the *Bhagavad Gītā*:

na hi jñānena sadrisham pavitramih vidyate.

Truly, there is nothing in this world as purifying as knowledge.

Vedanta, which contains the knowledge of eternal truths, is supreme among scriptures. It describes the four bodies (*sharira*) of the soul (*jīvātman*): the gross (*sthūla*), the subtle (*sukshma*), the causal (*karana*), and the supracausal (*mahākārana*). Vedanta explains that through *jñāna*, as the *sādhaka* is freed from the first three bodies one by one and reaches the fourth body—the transcendental state, the abode of the Self—he fully visualizes Lord Shiva, who is pure, nonattached, and *turīyātita* (beyond the fourth state). To understand the exact location, size, form, and nature of the different bodies is not at all easy. The soul's gross body is about five feet in size, is composed of five elementary constituents, and is red in color. The subtle body is about the size of a thumb, is white in color, and is located in the region of the throat. The causal body resides in the heart, is black in color, and is about half the size of the joint of the thumb. The fourth body is blue in color and about the size of a grain of lentil or a tiny spot. It is very difficult to be convinced of all this without a direct experience. Yet for a *japa yogi* there is no difficulty; it can be understood easily and naturally. This is because as one progresses in the practice of *japa*, one is gradually induced into a radiant state of *tandrā*, a superconscious state in which one is neither awake nor asleep. In *tandrā*, these bodies are clearly perceived.

When *japa* of the gross body, as recited by the tongue, goes deeper inside and begins to be repeated in the throat, it is known as *japa* of the subtle body. When this happens, the *sādhaka* should understand that *japa yoga* has purified the gross body and has now entered the subtle body. Here the number of mantra repetitions increases many times. During *japa* in the throat, the *sādhaka* experiences a divine *tandrā*. In this state he experiences a kind of blissful sleep and sometimes has visions of gods, goddesses, the Guru, and other Siddhas and saints. This second body, also called *sukshma sthāna*, is where dreams take place. By *japa* in the subtle body one's faith in *japa yoga* deepens, and now and again one feels happy within the heart. The reward that one gets from repeating the mantra a hundred times in the gross body, in a wakeful state, can be obtained by one repetition of the mantra in the subtle body. The *sādhaka* at this stage enjoys excellent health and lightness of body. Certain inner activities occur in the regions of the heart and navel. The *japa* of the throat goes on continuously day and night, like a fine stream of oil. It can be practiced by the *sādhaka* even while he attends to his daily, routine work. When *japa* is going on in the subtle body, the *sādhaka* quite naturally does all his work with skill and ability, for he receives guidance or inspiration from within. He even has a glimpse of the third (causal) body, which is black. In the final stage, *japa* in the subtle body enables the *sādhaka* to glimpse a number of things in his inner being, and these glimpses or revelations are significant.

When the subtle body is thoroughly purified, *japa* goes still deeper. Now it occurs in the heart, which is the location of the causal body. This region is also known as *sushupti sthāna*, or the seat of deep sleep. Some even call it *shunya sthāna*, or the void. That the causal body resides in the heart is the experience of all. The knot of ignorance (*hridayagranthi*) is also in this region. The seeds of all the evils that cause one to go round and round in the cycle of birth and death are also there. When *japa* is being repeated in the third body, the *sādhaka* becomes aware of the subtle vibrations of the syllables of the mantra. Now he is even more cheerful and enthusiastic than before and performs *japa* with increased love.

The number of mantra repetitions here is also more than those in the region of the throat. Here one repetition is equal to one hundred in the throat region. The *japa* of the heart region is very powerful. It not only strengthens the body and adds luster to the eyes and the face, but also makes the *sādhaka* do adventurous things. During *japa* in the heart, the heat increases in the head and the *sādhaka* feels warmth in all his limbs. Usually, he falls asleep during *japa*, yet the repetition of mantra maintains its continuity. Even when the *sādhaka* is busy with worldly work, *japa* continues internally. At this stage, he feels detached from everything and therefore attains proficiency in any work he undertakes.

When the required number of mantra repetitions of the third body is completed, *japa* moves to the navel region. From the spiritual point of view the navel region is of great importance. When *japa* moves to this region, the blue, lustrous fourth body is perceived within. During this stage, the *sādhaka* experiences various visions of divine lights. The light of the fourth body is indicative of the vision of God. This is also the light of Brahman, sometimes described as the supreme light of *japa*. Seeing this light, the *sādhaka* becomes very contented, hopeful, and enthusiastic and devotes more time to his spiritual endeavor. At this stage, the different states of *jñāna*, *bhakti*, and *yoga* arise. As soon as all the impurities such as desire and attachment are burned up in the fire of *japa* of the navel region, the *sādhaka* has visions of Siddhas, Gurus, gods and other heavenly beings, sacred rivers like the Ganges, the sun, moon, and other luminous bodies, and holy places like Shri Shailam, all in the state of *tandrā*. Naturally, with all these experiences he feels very hopeful of attaining the spiritual goal of ultimate fulfillment.

During *sādhanā* in the fourth body, the vibrations of *japa* are also felt in the head. By the power of *japa* in the navel region, all the hidden *shaktis* are awakened. Then, as a result of *japa*, the divine sound (*nāda*) is heard in the head, and the *sādhaka* listens to it with great wonder. At this stage, as a gift from the Guru, the *sādhaka* receives a sort of mantra in the form of continuous awareness of his own Self (*svasvarūpa-anusandhāna*). This mantra is a kind of medal from the benign and gracious Guru. Since the *sādhaka* has carried out his spiritual practices with unflinching faith and reached the fourth abode of *japa* through the strength of *gurukripā*, and because he has fulfilled the purpose for which he was initiated, the Guru is highly pleased. Therefore, in token of his delight and as a tribute to the disciple's worthiness, he gives a mantra which enables the disciple to realize his real Self. Immediately thereafter, the disciple is entirely transformed. Now *japa* is practiced through the unmanifest speech. The *sādhaka* does not have to make any effort to do this *japa*; it goes on automatically by the Guru's grace. This kind of *japa* is described as *ajapā-japa*, which the *sādhaka* joyfully listens to with a quiet, calm mind. Kabir expressed his own experience of this effortless *japa*:

> *hamārā japa kar rām,*
> *hama baithe ārām.*

Rama practices my *japa* while I sit relaxed.

For this *japa*, one has neither to move the tongue nor to make any attempt at focusing the mind, and there is neither hardship nor even weariness.

The *ajapā-japa*, or the *japa* of the fourth body, is actually neither *japa* nor action nor any kind of spiritual practice. At this stage the *sādhaka* feels, "I am perfect," and this feeling comes naturally to him. This *japa* is *nirgunanirākāra*, which means that it has no particular form or quality. There is no differentiation such as God and devotee, yoga and yogi, or mantra and reciter. Instead, there is a blissful feeling of indivisible unity with the universe. Just as a king feels, "This is my kingdom," wherever he goes in his own territory; just as the sky hears its own echoes everywhere, in all directions; just as an actor, though playing various roles feels only himself in them; similarly, a *sādhaka* who has the awareness "I am perfect" sees his own Self pervading everything. This is the highest goal of *gurukripā*, the culminating fruit of *sādhanā*.

Such a blessed *sādhaka* loses his individuality. Initially, he perceived the world as full of misery and hardship and as a place of transient enjoyments. But when transformed by the practice of *japa yoga*, he has the experience that, being one with the Guru, he is ageless and immortal. To him the universe now appears to be a paradise, and the world, the Sadguru, and all fellow beings look benign like Shiva. In the vast garden of this universe, he proclaims, "I am Shiva," for, indeed, he has become Shiva. He neither loves nor hates, because for him all likes and dislikes have become Shiva, and the universe has become the form of Shiva. With the worshipful knowledge of the universe as Lord Shiva, he cheerfully fulfills his remaining *prārabdha*. Constantly practicing the *japa* of unity, he enters the holiest region of the fourth body; transcending even the fourth state, that is, becoming *turīyātita*, he realizes that only he and nothing else exists. Just as one who is on the ocean sees nothing except water on all sides, similarly, a *japa yogi*, devoid of the feeling of mine and yours, interior and exterior, higher and lower, sees only his own Self everywhere.

"I am Shiva. There is nothing different from Shiva, nothing other than Shiva"—thus convinced that I, you, he, and all are Shiva, and merging in Shiva, Shiva becomes Shiva. This is *japa yoga's* highest reward; this is the pinnacle of Guru's grace; this is the final result of the *sādhaka's* spiritual fortitude; this is religion put into practice; this is visiting the holiest Shiva temple of Kailas on one's pilgrimage to ultimate liberation.

That the *sādhaka* has all these different experiences, that he has a vision of the Guru and even converses with him in the blue *mahākārana*, or fourth body, is not an exaggeration. The unmanifest speech, which spontaneously arises in the fourth body, is *chitimāyā*, that is, pure Consciousness. Chiti Shakti is entirely independent. The *Pratyabhijñāhridayam* says, *chitiḥ svatantrā vishvasiddhihetuḥ*, "Supremely independent Chiti is the cause of the manifestation of the universe."

Chiti, the nonseparable soul power of the Supreme Shiva, is independently powerful. She is the cause of the creation, sustenance, and dissolution of the world, from the highest being to the inert, insentient earth. Chiti governs all the activities of the entire universe. There is nothing beyond or higher than Chiti, the Absolute Consciousness; nor is She different from Supreme Shiva. The universe comes into existence because of Her unfolding, and when She turns inward in the process of involution, the universe dissolves. Chiti is the cause of the entire objective world, and Chiti is also the fulfillment of all endeavors. Chiti is the substratum of the universe. The world, both the visible and the invisible, is created by Chiti without any material or instrumental cause. Chiti Herself takes the form of the universe, but Her innate nature as pure Consciousness does not change. Without the help of any object or any other power, Chiti alone and independently carries out Her work; She assumes infinite forms and creates the universe. Just as the various organs of the physical body are formed from one drop of semen, just as the fruit, flower, and leaf of the entire banyan tree lie hidden in its one small seed, in the same way this Chiti displays a sort of grand dance in the universe. By becoming both cause and effect and by donning universal and individual form, She enjoys Her greatness perpetually.

With such power, it is not difficult for the Chiti Shakti to appear in a *sādhaka's* visions, assuming various forms and guiding him as well. Therefore, what a *sādhaka* sees outside in the world he also sees within himself, because the individual body is the form of the universe. The direct experience of a *sādhaka* is the only proof of the validity of this truth.

It is invariably true that the Guru, in a subtle form, resides in the two-petaled lotus located between a *sādhaka's* eyebrows. The Guru is in fact the same as the grace-bestowing Chiti that pervades the universe. When the required number of mantra repetitions is completed at this center, the Guru gives the *sādhaka* a mantra within the fourth body. No matter where the disciple may be staying, it is very easy for the Chiti Shakti to appear to him in a vision in the form of his own Guru. This is neither an overestimation of Her power, nor a figment of imagination, nor even magic.

My revered Gurudev, Bhagawan Shri Nityananda, used to guide his devotees in far-off countries such as England and America. Once he even gave guidance in a vision to a man traveling by plane. The Chiti Shakti is unfathomable in Her potency and full of infinite miracles. At any time, under any circumstances (favorable or otherwise), Chiti assumes marvelous forms of many in one or of one in many. Depending on a *sādhaka*'s sincerity, faith, and confidence, supereminent Chiti makes him fearless and, according to his feelings and understanding, even instructs and guides him assuming the form of the Guru.

When a yogi reaches the highest realm of yoga, his awakened Kundalini, having united with Shiva in the *sahasrāra*, penetrates and becomes diffused in every nerve, every cell, and every hair of his body. Thus, when the Kundalini has completely pervaded the four bodies, the five concentric sheaths (of physical matter, vital energy, mind, intelligence, and bliss), and the three states (waking, dreaming, and deep sleep), She firmly stabilizes the yogi's insight in realizing oneness everywhere. The *Shiva Sūtras* say, *yathā atra tathā anyatra*, which means that what is here is everywhere. To the yogi, therefore, any place is the same. For him heaven, earth, and the netherworld, Paris, London, New York, and Tokyo, China, Russia, and Tibet are all one—Shiva's empire.

Once a disciple of such a yogi was doing the *sādhanā* of meditation in America and running a business at the same time. This *sādhaka* was in urgent need of some spiritual guidance. One day when he sat for meditation, his Guru appeared and instructed him in English. The disciple was extremely pleased that his Guru was so great. He wrote a letter to us stating that his Guru, the great yogi, visited him in America and, after hav-

ing had a good talk with him, returned to India. I replied that
this was no cause for surprise. Such phenomena occur through
the Chiti Shakti, which equally and fully pervades everywhere.

Chiti, the supreme power, knows all languages. All knowledge, all science, all wisdom are the creations of Her vibrations.
The science of yoga, together with all its branches, is merely a
small particle of Chiti's infinite being. Chiti is in all respects the
Guru, the Master, of every religious and spiritual path. Molding
Herself in an approachable form, she instructs and guides a *sādha-
ka* in the language that he understands. It is not at all difficult for
Her to do so. Although the world, consisting of movable and
immovable things, is the same in the form of the divine Shakti,
She makes the *sādhaka* see the same in an infinite variety.

From the same condensed milk a variety of sweets, of different shapes, colors, and flavors, are prepared. A variety of figures
are painted by an artist on the same canvas, with the same brush
and the same color. Onlookers may distinguish them as pictures
of a man, a child, a cow, a horse, a flower, and a fruit, but in truth
the artist is one, the canvas is one, the color is one, and the brush
is one. The artist has no feeling of good or bad toward any figure. He believes that he has painted many in one. To paint a new
figure or to erase a painted one raises no question of either like
or dislike, delight, sorrow, or anxiety. Similarly, the divine Chiti
creates the world of infinite forms by Her own power, without
any particular motive or expectation.

This mysterious Chiti, taking the form of a mantra, resides
in the syllables of the mantra. Therefore, such mantras are Chiti
Herself. As a *sādhaka* practices more and more mantra *japa*,
Chiti burns up his feeling of limited individuality in the fire of
mantra and elevates him to the experience of oneness with the
infinite Self. Since mantra is Chiti, it also has Chiti's capacity for
creation, sustenance, and dissolution. The truth of all this can be
known only through Self-realization.

However much one may say or write on the subject of
mantra japa, it will always remain incomplete, for there is no
end to it. *Japa* gives shelter to all; there are no barriers to its prac-

tice; and through it the desired ends, powers, and perfection can be achieved. Through *japa*, liberation is attained in this very life. *Japa* is divine and the practitioner of *japa* attains divinity. *Japa* leads to the highest fulfillment.

CHAPTER SIX

THE PATH OF KNOWLEDGE

Self-realization is not attained without knowledge, for knowledge is the very nature of God. The Supreme Being blazes forth as knowledge. Without knowledge it is not possible to have the final experience. God, in fact, is ever present within our inner being. He pervades the entire universe, sentient as well as insentient. He always shines in the heart. It is God who makes our minds active. Although He has always been with us, we are still ignorant of Him. Therefore, our need for knowledge is great.

If the nature of the inner Self is knowledge, why do we not immediately perceive the Self? Our inner Self is undecaying, perfect, eternal, and self-effulgent—then why are we in such a plight? Why have we not discovered our own nature? What has rendered the ever-enlightened ignorant, Consciousness matter, the perfect imperfect, and the blissful miserable?

The cause of all this is ignorance. Because of our own ignorance, we have shrunk from sublimity to pettiness, from infinity to finitude, from wholeness to fragmentation. When our ignorance is completely eradicated, we become fully enlightened. Just as night can be ended by day alone, cold by heat, and sins by virtuous deeds, so ignorance can be destroyed only by knowledge. *Japa*, austerities, fasting, sacrifices, and other rituals cannot dispel ignorance completely. It is knowledge that fully reveals the nature of God. The light of the soul is indeed the light of knowledge.

Where are you looking for God — God who is eternally present in all places, all moments of time, and all things? In what corners are you searching for the One who is ever-existent? It is all right to strive to obtain something that you do not have or that exists in a remote region. But how can you seek that which you always have and which is the closest, the innermost? In which holy place, cave, or forest retreat can you find Him? Manpuri said:

kyom bana-bana dhūmdhata sāīm,
sāīm ghata māhīm,
koī puraba koī pashchima,
guru bina upajata nāhīm.

Why are you looking for God from forest to forest when He exists within the heart? One looks for Him in the east, another in the west, but He cannot be seen without the Guru.

I, too, searched intensely for Him in caves, mountains, and forests. But when I came to Bhagawan Nityananda, I perceived Him at once. I do not remember in exactly how many temples I had sought Him or in how many shrines I had meditated on Him to no avail. I prayed in so many different temples, but only hours slipped by and I was still without peace. I practiced severe austerities, but they only emaciated my body without taking me closer to God. I practiced *pranāyāma* and struggled with other *hatha yoga* techniques for a prolonged period, but I only became proud that I was a good yogi; I did not obtain peace. I constantly repeated the divine name. I sang devotional songs — even with professional singers — until I was weary. I told beads, put the sacred mark on my forehead, and let my hair grow into matted locks. But all that I had were the beads, the sacred mark, and the long locks. Time passed without any real gain.

Then I set out in search of a guide. One naked one turned out to be addicted to the pipe, while another asked me to pierce my ears in the Shaivite manner. One told me to smear my body with sacred ash, another to wear a black garment. Yet another suggested saffron robes. One instructed me to observe silence. Thus, my search continued until I was exhausted. Then I wandered all by myself, pondering the mysteries of life. In the course of those wanderings, I ran into an unusual, naked saint named Zipruanna. He was very great. Although he appeared to be a fool to worldly minded fools, he was omniscient. He seemed a naked mendicant only to those who were spiritually naked, being without knowledge. However, he was the owner of a vast treasure of wisdom—a true millionaire. I loved him at first sight. We became friends. What a combination! One was a naked *fakir* while the other was a well-dressed, modern renunciant. He said, "O you crazy one, God is within! Why do you seek Him outside?"

I said, "Instruct me."

"That is not for me to do," he replied. "Go to Ganeshpuri. Your treasure lies there. Go and claim it."

I went to Ganeshpuri and met Nityananda Baba, the supreme *avadhūta*. I was overjoyed. No—I was fulfilled. After a bath in the hot springs, I went for his *darshan*. He was poised in a simple, easy posture on a plain cot, smiling gently. His eyes were in the *shambavi mudrā* (eyes open but gaze directed within). What divine luster glowed in those eyes! His body was dark, and he was wearing a simple loincloth. He said, "So you've come."

"Yes, Sir," I answered. I stood for a while and then sat down. There I realized the highest. I am still sitting there. Where shall I go now?

Peace cannot be had in the absence of the Guru, nor can self-contentment or inspiration. When I obtained Sadguru Nityananda, I obtained all.

Nityananda said, "Why look for the indwelling Lord outside? Look within your own being. Your Rama, your peace, lies inside. Meditate."

Through meditation I received the Guru's grace, and then I found Him easily. He whom I had been seeking in holy centers, caves, forests, mantras, and robes was disclosed by my Guru to be my own Self, seated in my own heart.

Thus, God cannot be realized without the Guru even though He is manifest. Therefore, obtain true vision from the Guru and you will see Him. The Lord showed Himself to Arjuna as being present in his own heart. If someone were to ask me what Krishna gave to Arjuna, I would say that the Lord, in His role as the supreme Guru, granted Arjuna the eye of knowledge. Krishna dwelled within Arjuna, but because Arjuna lacked the eye of wisdom, he could not see Him who was his own all-pervading Self. As a result he had neither peace nor courage. When he received the inner eye from the Guru, he at once discovered God in his own heart.

Friends, do not seek God; seek the Guru. God abides within you. The Guru is the one you need to grant you the divine vision of the inner light. And that divine vision is the highest knowledge. *Yoga*, devotion, *japa*, and austerities cannot equal it. But it must be directly revealed by the Guru. Mere words are of no avail. It is the direct, immediate experience that alone matters. Without knowledge you cannot get anywhere. Lose the ego and find the Self. Merge your separate existence into the Universal Being. Then you will find peace stretching infinitely on all sides.

You will see very little if you merely close your eyes and begin to search. You will only complain that it is all dark. But the truth is that it is all light. It is only your eyes that are blind. In fact, all those who try to see without the eye of knowledge are blind. Behold the inner witness, the spectator who watches all the activities of your waking state while remaining apart from them; who dwells in the midst of all action, good or bad, knowing it fully and yet remaining uncontaminated by it; who is that supremely pure, perfect, and ever-unattached Being. Try to know Him who does not sleep during the state of sleep, remaining fully aware and witnessing all the events of the dream world. On waking up one may say, "I slept very well. I had a dream about a beautiful temple." Are these words uttered by the one who slept? He says that he saw a temple while he slept! What an enigma! O friends, behold the spectator who remains awake while you sleep, poised far from sleep. Who is He? He is the pure witness, the attributeless One. He is the Supreme Being. He is within you, but you look for Him outside.

Human beings have four bodies, one within the other. They should be explored. What exists in the fourth body? That is the realm of pure Consciousness, of the beloved Self delighting in itself—the land of perfect contentment, of total freedom from anxiety, of the highest realization. Plunge within through meditation, surveying the inner territory with the eye of knowledge. Nanakdev said:

> *bāhara bhītara eka hī jāno,*
> *yaha guru jñāna batāī.*

The same One pervades within and without. This has been revealed by the knowledge received from the Guru.

It is true that what is inside is also outside. Explore it for yourself. Consider an analogy: The earth is present everywhere. Wherever you go, you remain on its surface. Similarly, the world is in God and God is in the world. Where are you looking for Him? Why do you exhaust yourself unnecessarily? Your penance is futile. You only become weary in your search for Him. You are picking up cow dung for nothing.

An aspirant once approached a Guru and said, "Venerable Master, I take refuge in you. Please instruct me."

This saint was a simple person with an all-pervading outlook. He said, "Thou art That—God dwells within you."

"I know this already," the student said. "Please teach me something more."

The teacher replied, "Brother, I have only one teaching. If you want a different teaching you will have to find a different teacher."

The seeker went away in search of another Master. This time he approached a great one who had attained full knowledge, having mastered the science of the Absolute and gained a direct experience of it. The Master was sitting in silence. The seeker said, "Sir, kindly impart knowledge to me. I am without any knowledge of the Self."

The Master asked, "Where have you come from?"

The seeker told him the name of his earlier teacher. As soon as the Master heard the name, he realized that without service, knowledge imparted to this seeker would never bear fruit. So he said, "You will have to serve the Guru for twelve years. Then you will receive true knowledge."

The seeker accepted this condition and said, "Knowledge is all I want. Please tell me in what manner I may serve you."

The Master called the manager of the ashram and asked, "Is there a vacant job in the ashram?"

The manager said, "All the work is going well. There is only one job available, and that is picking up cow dung."

The Master told the seeker, "You may have the job of picking up cow dung. At the end of twelve years, at the consummation of service, you will obtain knowledge."

The seeker picked up dung and cleaned the cowshed every day. After twelve years had gone by, he went to the Master and said, "Gurudev, I have completed my service. Grant me knowledge now."

The Guru said, "Thou art That. All that there is, is the Self, and it is you."

When he heard this, the seeker was satisfied. He had no doubt about the truth of the Guru's words. Yet he asked, "I knew this before; I even heard it explained. Why, then, did you make me pick up cow dung?"

The Guru replied, "Your experience should answer your question. Since you performed *guruseva* for twelve years with faith and devotion, you now understand these words. It is the reward for your service."

The world is as one sees it. It reflects one's own state. If the world is regarded as real in itself, it becomes filled with sorrow, misery, want, and anxiety. The world appears to be mundane because of one's own ignorance of the play of the Spirit. The world deceives us when we consider it to be simply the world as we see it. However, once we experience the blissful sport of Consciousness, the world is transformed into a haven of bliss.

Because of our ignorance of the nature of a rope, we actually perceive it as a serpent. If we see the rope as a rope, our perception is true and our peace is not disturbed. We remain happy and without fear. But if we see wrongly, we see the serpent and fall victim to fear and agitation.

A person becomes his own enemy and begins to torture himself. He himself becomes a sinner and then groans. He himself serves the poison of ignorance to himself and thus commits suicide. While he is hostile to himself, he blames others. Why do you commit suicide for lack of knowledge? Give up your illusions and see yourself as you really are. Uplift yourself by means of knowledge. Serve the nectar of wisdom to yourself. Achieve greatness. The soul dwells as the perceiving Consciousness in every being. Reflect on the inner Truth. Explore your own depths. Direct your seeking within. Revel in your own being.

The poet Ramchandra told a story which illustrates that one becomes what one thinks. Its meaning is profound. Whatever one wishes for under the *kalpavriksha* (the wish-fulfilling tree) one gets. Once a slothful, foolish, and destitute fellow approached this tree. Finding it shady and beautiful, he sat under it. The surroundings were fascinating. The man began to wish, "If only there were a bungalow here!" Immediately a bungalow appeared. "If only there were a garden around it!" A garden also appeared. Then followed cushions, pillows, and beds. A kitchen, equipped with gold and silver utensils, also materialized and then a table covered with sweet delicacies. "If only there were a woman here!" the man thought. And at once a beautiful maiden came along.

Then this dull-witted fool began to think, "Whatever I wish for comes into being. Can there possibly be a devil around?" As soon as he entertained this thought, a frightful devil appeared. The fellow was scared out of his wits. He began to think, "Most likely this devil will eat me up!" Immediately the devil pounced on him and devoured him.

O dear ones! This world is not a vale of sorrow. It is neither a transient phenomenon nor a void. It is neither a field of action nor illusory, neither real nor unreal nor an abode of differences. It is the beautiful playground of Lord Shiva; it is not inert matter but the divine abode of gods. To the ignorant and blind it is transitory, but to the enlightened, to those filled with devotion to the Guru, it is the sport of the Absolute. For the unbelieving, the world is a vale of tears, but for the believing and detached who are filled with love for God, it is the manifestation of His love. For the wise, for perfect and ecstatic beings, this world is a divine, intoxicated play. Know the world fully; know it as it is. Do not confuse a post with a thief and run around in sheer panic. Do not become trapped in the performance of naming and sacred-thread ceremonies. Do not consider this divine play to be the son of a barren woman. Do not get ready for a bath with soap and towel, regarding as real the waters of a mirage. The world, in fact, is Shiva; it is Kailas; it is Rama. This indeed is Vaikuntha. This world is an expansion of the highest Shiva, a conscious playground of the love of universal Consciousness. It is nothing but Chiti. You, He, and I are all permeated with Chiti. Whatever is, is Chiti. Look with this all-embracing vision, the vision of knowledge. What nectars flow here! Look at the beauty of the beloved Universal Mother.

Understanding is determined by knowledge. Attitude is shaped by understanding. Peace and joy arise in the mind according to one's attitude. Take the case of an ordinary soldier. If he becomes a lieutenant, he feels more important. As he rises through the ranks from a lieutenant to a major and then to a brigadier general and finally assumes the position of commander-in-chief, his power increases progressively and so does his awareness of his stature. If he becomes the president of his country, his authority is far more pervasive and he also feels far more important. Actually this person remains the same throughout. What changes then? It is his own idea of himself. He felt insignificant while he was a soldier, but now he considers himself not a soldier but the president of his country. Similarly, if you give up the wrong view of yourself as a trivial, destitute, inferior, begging, and imprisoned creature and instead begin to feel that you are Shiva, the all-pervasive soul, that you are perfection itself, how much greater your joy will be! Stop looking upon yourself as a limited individual. Become firmly anchored in the sense of your own pervasiveness, of your ability, greatness, and purity.

Bhagawan Nityananda used to say, "All are Rama—great as well as small. Rama is yours. Rama is mine." This is truly the essence of Vedanta. He had seen the mystery of things. He was fully aware of the inner observer, the one who understands. His skill in practical affairs was based on the Vedantic vision of unity in diversity. Sometimes he would say, "Neither go toward another or move away from him. Neither become hostile to anyone or run to strike up friendships. Do not rush to accept a gift or become entangled in the pride of giving. Do not look for faults in others, or congratulate yourself on singing their praises. Shun evil completely, but do not at the same time become attached to good. Every moment utter, 'O Rama! O Rama!' Never forget Rama. Think of God and not of yourself. Regarding praise and blame as brothers, continue to repeat, 'O Rama! O Rama!' Destitution should be as welcome as riches. Both of them are the fruits of past actions. They affect one who identifies himself with them. Remain detached from both since they are the consequences of destiny determined by *karma* and are the will of God. Do not prefer one to the other, and thus avoid being pseudo-wise. Do not set yourself up as a worthless middleman who snatches from the rich and distributes to the poor. Do not become agitated by either the riches of the wealthy or the poverty of the poor. Constantly utter, 'O Rama! O Rama! O Rama!'

"Putting on the guise of the love of Rama, you claim to be a follower of Rama, yet you resort to the malicious distinction of high and low. Open your eye of knowledge and see what you should do. You have sought initiation in the outlook of equality, but your actions reek of partisanship, of inequality. This is a mockery of devotion and knowledge. Do not behave like this. It is Rama who appears in different guises. Continually repeat, 'O Rama! O Rama!'

"This world is Rama's playhouse. There cannot be a king without subjects. There cannot be riches without poverty. There cannot be day without night. The universe is based on duality. Duality will vanish only when the universe vanishes. O renunciant, why have you given up repeating the name of Rama and turned to other things instead? Why should you take sides in any way? Realize that it is Rama who weeps and Rama who laughs. Why do you abandon the name of Rama? Keep repeating the divine name of Rama. Rama's will alone works. Much of your life has already been spent fruitlessly. Not much time is left before you die. Why do you perceive differences in Rama? All is Rama; all is Rama indeed."

This is what Nityananda Baba used to say. His teaching embodied the essence of Vedanta, embracing unity in diversity and diversity in unity. Let your understanding be enlightened by Vedanta or you will be subject to remorse.

Once an extremely kind person went to a sage and began to talk to him about a plan he had devised to abolish poverty. The sage told him, "Brother, this world is dominated by the law of *karma*. When did God entrust you with the task of changing it?" He added, "Just as wealth is an illusion, so is poverty. Friend, repeat every moment, 'O Rama! O Rama!'"

Do not forget that Self-knowledge, or God-realization, is your aim. Some people turn away from practical life under the illusion that it is an obstacle on the path to God. But later they unwittingly get caught in the same trap. It is very difficult to escape the net of past impressions. A holy pretender is not even aware of how his holiness betrays him, how it makes him conceited, thus plunging him into ignorance. Ordinarily it is exceedingly difficult to save oneself without the grace of the Supreme Sadguru. Generally a so-called wise devotee gradually loses his wisdom when he has to apply it to worldly affairs. To one with the eye of devotion, all are Gopal. Kings, millionaires, the poor, the foolish, soldiers, poets, actors, and artists—all these are only different players in the divine drama. One's outer form or circumstances are determined by one's *karma*. However, for a devotee, the enjoyment of objects in the external world does not bring him closer to Rama. He finds Rama only when he is absorbed in the inner Self. Indifferent to riches as well as poverty, both of which are barren and joyless, he keeps his attention focused on his Self reposing in his heart. A true worshiper of Rama's name is so absorbed in divine love and knowledge that he does not attach any importance to the wealth of the entire universe or to that of the worlds of Brahma, heaven, Indra, or the moon. Equanimity, perfection, friendship with his own Self, courtesy arising from the awareness of the Self in all, and nobility of character constitute his true wealth. To see distinction in knowledge and devotion is nothing but party politics. Love and knowledge will survive only if they are kept apart from politics; otherwise, they will die.

The Vedantic philosophy of equality is based on true vision. Pleasure and pain, gain and loss, wealth and poverty are all consequences of *karma*. They pertain only to the gross body, whereas insight is the transcendental wealth of the supracausal body. How can those without knowledge and devotion, those who are slaves of money, outer honors, degrees, and titles, obtain this wealth? O renunciant, turn away from the external world and plunge within. There lies your true kingdom. You are the emperor of transcendental realms. Try to rise above the illusion of differences. Acquire the vision of oneness, of sages, seers, and other enlightened beings—the vision of pure knowledge, the vision of the divine play. Be guided by the pure Vedantic insight, by the experience of transcendental bliss, and by the knowledge of the true nature of God. It is only this vision of unity that enables one to realize the Godhead, that puts an end to human suffering, and that raises human beings to the divine plane. If you become the sovereign of your own inner kingdom and are led by divine inspiration, you will see Rama everywhere. You will see Shyam stretching from east to west, and Shiva from north to south. This is the kingdom of *avadhūtas*, the boundless expanse of pure joy. Obtain this treasure at this very moment. It is the strong and beautiful abode of bliss. Let your mind be focused on it. This is the goal of the knowledge of the enlightened, of the devotion of devotees, of the meditation of meditators—the true imperishable state that is worth attaining. This is truly the gift of the grace of Sadguru Nityananda.

Swami Muktananda

SWAMI MUKTANANDA
and the Lineage of Siddha Yoga Masters

Swami Muktananda was born in 1908 to a prosperous family of landowners near the South Indian city of Mangalore. At around the age of fifteen, he had several encounters with the great saint, Bhagawan Nityananda, whom he would later recognize as his spiritual Master. These encounters were a turning point for the boy. Shortly thereafter, he decided to set out from home in search of direct experience of God, a journey that would ultimately take him three times across the length and breadth of India and last almost a quarter of a century. He met his first teacher, Siddharudha Swami, who was one of the renowned scholars and saints of that time, in an ashram in Hubli, two hundred miles to the north of his parents' home. It was there that he studied Vedanta, took the vows of *sannyāsa*, or monkhood, and received the name Swami Muktananda, "the bliss of liberation."

When Siddharudha died, in 1929, Swami Muktananda began to visit one ashram after another, meeting and learning from more than sixty spiritual teachers, always looking for the one who would give him the experience of God. He searched for eighteen years. In that time he mastered the major scriptures of India, received training in an array of disciplines and skills—from hatha yoga to cooking and Ayurvedic medicine—and still he did not find what he sought.

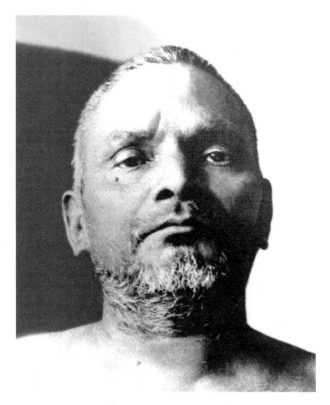

Bhagawan Nityananda

At last one of the saints he met sent him to Bhagawan Nityananda, the Siddha Master, or perfected spiritual teacher, he had encountered so many years before. Bhagawan Nityananda was then living in the tiny village of Ganeshpuri, fifty miles northeast of Bombay. Recognizing Bhagawan Nityananda as the Guru he had been seeking, Swami Muktananda later said that this meeting "ended my wandering forever." From Bhagawan Nityananda he received *shaktipāt*, the sacred initiation of the Siddhas by which one's inner spiritual energy is awakened. This energy, known as *kundalinī*, is a divine potential that exists within each human being; once awakened, it enables a seeker to reach the most subtle levels of inner experience.

With his initiation, Swami Muktananda became a disciple, dedicating himself to the spiritual path set forth by his Guru. This was the beginning of nine years of intense transformation, during which Muktananda underwent total purification, explored the inner realms of consciousness, and finally became steady in his experience of the fullness and ecstasy of his own innermost nature. In 1956 Bhagawan Nityananda declared that his disciple's inner journey was complete: Swami Muktananda had attained Self-realization, the experience of union with God.

Even after he had attained the goal of his discipleship, Swami Muktananda remained a devoted disciple, continuing to live quietly near Ganeshpuri. Bhagawan Nityananda established him in a small ashram near his own, and for five years, Guru and disciple lived less than a mile from each other. Then in 1961, just before his death, Bhagawan Nityananda passed on to Swami Muktananda the grace-bestowing power of the Siddha Masters, investing him with the capacity to give spiritual awakening to others. On that day, Bhagawan Nityananda told him, "The entire world will see you."

In the decades that followed, Baba, as Swami Muktananda came to be known, traveled throughout the world, imparting to others the same shaktipat initiation he himself had received and introducing seekers to the spontaneous yoga of the Siddha Masters. He freely bestowed the grace his Guru had given to him, opening to unprecedented numbers of people what he called "the royal road" of Siddha Yoga—a wide and accessible path to God. People who had never before heard of meditation found that in Baba's presence they were drawn into an inner stillness that gave their lives new focus and meaning. He introduced programs to give shaktipat initiation to vast groups and tirelessly explained to people the ongoing process of transformation that was unfolding within them. As Baba became world renowned, his ashram (now known as Gurudev Siddha Peeth) expanded to accommodate the visiting seekers, and in time other ashrams and hundreds of Siddha Yoga meditation centers were established throughout the world.

In 1982, shortly before his death, Swami Muktananda designated Swami Chidvilasananda his successor. She had been his disciple since early childhood and had traveled with him since 1973, translating into English his writings, his lectures, and the many informal exchanges he had with his devotees. An advanced spiritual seeker from an early age, with a great longing for God, she became an exemplary disciple. She was guided meticulously in her *sādhanā* by her Guru, who carefully prepared her to succeed him as Guru. In early May of 1982, Swami Chidvilasananda took formal vows of monkhood, and later that month Swami Muktananda bequeathed to her the power and authority of the Siddha lineage, the same spiritual legacy that his Guru had passed on to him. Since that time, Gurumayi, as she is widely known, has given shaktipat and taught the practices of Siddha Yoga to ever-increasing numbers of seekers, introducing them to Swami Muktananda's message:

> *Meditate on your Self.*
> *Honor your Self.*
> *Worship your Self.*
> *Understand your own Self.*
> *God dwells within you as you.*

Gurumayi Chidvilasananda

GLOSSARY

Āchārya
A teacher.

Advaita Vedanta
The philosophy of absolute nondualism, one of the six orthodox schools of Indian philosophy, expressed in the Upanishads and other texts that consider the nature of the Self.

Apāna
Inhalation. *See also Prāna.*

Āsana
(1) Any one of various bodily postures practiced to strengthen the body, purify the nerves, and develop one-pointedness of mind. The yoga texts describe eighty-four major *āsanas.* (2) A seat or mat on which one sits for meditation. *See also Ashtānga Yoga.*

Ashtānga Yoga
The eightfold yoga, also known as *raja yoga,* expounded by the sage Patanjali in his *Yoga Sūtras.* The eight steps are: (1) *yamas:* the practice of five moral virtues—nonviolence, truthfulness, celibacy, nonstealing, and noncovetousness; (2) *niyamas:* the practice of five regular habits—purity, contentment, austerity, study, and surrender; (3) *āsana:*

posture; (4) *prānāyāma:* the regulation and restraint of the breath; (5) *pratyāhāra:* withdrawal of the mind from sense objects; (6) *dhāranā:* concentration, fixing the mind on an object of contemplation; (7) *dhyāna:* meditation, the continuous flow of thoughts toward one object; (8) *samādhi:* complete absorption or identification with the object of meditation, meditative union with the Absolute.

Ātman
See Self.

Avadhūta
A great being and renunciant who has risen above duality and whose behavior is not bound by ordinary social conventions.

Bhagavad Gītā
One of the world's greatest works of spiritual literature, in which Lord Krishna explains the path of liberation to his disciple Arjuna. The *Bhagavad Gītā* is part of the Sanskrit epic, the *Mahābhārata.*

Bhakti
Divine love; devotion to God.

Chaitanya
The fundamental Consciousness.

Chakra

(*lit.* wheel) Any one of the major energy centers, or subtle nerve plexus, in the human body.

Darshan

(*lit.*, to see) (1) The direct experience of God; the perception of the Truth in the presence of a holy being or image of God. (2) The various spiritual philosophies of India are known as *darshanas.*

Dhāranā

See Ashtānga Yoga.

Dhyāna

Meditation. *See also Ashtānga Yoga.*

Eknath Maharaj

(1528-1609) A householder poet-saint of Maharashtra, India, and disciple of Janardan Swami. By writing on religious subjects in the vernacular, Eknath ushered in a spiritual revival.

Ganeshpuri

A village north of Bombay in Maharashtra, India, near Gurudev Siddha Peeth, the main ashram of Siddha Yoga.

Gurubhakta

One who follows the path of devotional love for the Guru.

Gurudev Siddha Peeth

The main ashram of Siddha Yoga, located near the village of Ganeshpuri in Maharashtra, India.

Hanuman

(*lit.* heavy-jawed) A devotee of Lord Rama who was the perfect servant, his story is told in the *Rāmāyana* epic. His form is that of a monkey with extraordinary strength.

Indra

The Vedic lord of heaven.

Jnaneshwar Maharaj

(1275-1296) Foremost among the poet-saints of Maharashtra, India, and author of the *Jñāneshwarī,* the great commentary on the *Bhagavad Gītā* in the Marathi language, one of the treasures of world spiritual literature.

Kabir

(1440-1518) A great poet-saint and mystic who lived his life as a simple weaver, and whose influence was a powerful force in overcoming the fierce religious factionalism of the day. His poems are still being studied and sung all over the world.

Kailas

A peak in the Himalayas, regarded as the abode of Shiva.

Kali Yuga

One of the four ages; the present "dark age," in which righteousness and truth have degenerated.

Kāmadhenu

The sage Vasishtha's cow, said to satisfy all desires.

Karma

The results of actions performed either in this life or in past lives. Past *karmas* form our current destiny. There are three categories of *karma*: *prārabdha karma,* destined to be played out in the current lifetime; *sanchita karma,* for future lifetimes, currently existing in seed form; and *kriyaman karma,* which is created in the present lifetime. The first type of *karma* unfolds even if one attains liberation in this lifetime; the latter two are burned up when liberation is attained.

Kriyā

A physical, mental, or emotional movement initiated by the awakened *kundalinī* for the purpose of purification. *See also Kundalinī.*

Kundalinī

(*lit.* coiled one) The supreme power or primordial energy that lies coiled at the base of the spine in a dormant state in every human being. When awakened, this extremely subtle force travels upward through the many channels of the subtle body, initiating various yogic practices that bring about the purification of the entire being. When *kundalinī* is fully unfolded, the individual self merges into the supreme Self, and the cycle of birth and death comes to an end.

Laya Yoga
Absorption of the mind into the Self; dissolution; the interiorization of consciousness.

Mahābhārata
The great epic poem in Sanskrit composed by the sage Vyasa, which recounts the war between the Pandava and the Kaurava brothers over a disputed kingdom. Its main theme is the nature of *dharma* or righteousness. Within this vast narrative is contained a wealth of Indian secular and religious lore.

Mahāvākya
Four statements containing the essence of the wisdom of the Upanishads. They are "Thou art That," "The Self is Brahman, the Absolute," "Consciousness is Brahman," and "I am Brahman."

Māyā
Illusion; the divine Power through which God appears as the world of names and forms.

Mudrā
(*lit,* seal) (1) Various advanced *hatha yoga* techniques practiced as aids to concentration to hold the *prāna* in the body, forcing the *kundalinī* to flow into the *sushumnā nādī.* Mudrās can occur spontaneously after receiving *shaktipāt.* (2) Symbolic gestures and movements of the hand expressing inner states.

Muni
An inspired sage or saint.

Nādīs
The channels in the subtle body through which the vital force flows. The main *nādī* is the *sushumnā,* the central channel through which the awakened *kundalinī* energy rises. *See also Kundalinī; Sushumnā Nādī.*

Nanakdev
(1469-1538) Also known as Guru Nanak. The founder and first Guru of the Sikh religion. He lectured widely, spreading liberal religious and social doctrines including opposition to both the caste system and the division between Hindus and Muslims.

Narada Bhakti Sūtras
The classic scripture on devotion composed by the sage Narada; also known as the philosophy of love.

Nirvikalpa
The highest state of *samādhi* beyond attribute, thought, or image. *See also Samādhi.*

Niyamas
See Ashtānga Yoga.

Om, Omkāra
The primal sound from which the entire universe emanates. It is the inner essence of all mantras.

Paramahamsa
One who has completely mastered all of his senses; one who has attained Self-realization.

Patanjali
A great fourth-century sage and the author of the *Yoga Sūtras,* the basic text on the eight limbs of the path of yoga, and the means of attaining *samādhi.*

Prāna
Exhalation; also, the vital life-sustaining force of the human body.

Prānāyāma
See Ashtānga Yoga.

Prārabdha Karma
See Karma.

Pratyabhijñāhridayam
(*lit,* the heart of the doctrine of recognition) A concise text of Kashmir Shaivism consisting of twenty *sūtras* composed by the sage Kshemaraja on the cosmic process of involution and evolution.

Pratyāhāra
See Ashtānga Yoga.

Puranas
(*lit,* ancient legends) Eighteen sacred books by the sage Vyasa containing stories, legends, and hymns about the creation of the universe, the incarnations of God, the teachings of various deities, and the spiritual legacies of ancient kings and sages.

Raja Yoga
See Ashtānga Yoga.

Rama
The seventh major incarnation of Lord Vishnu, the sustaining power of the universe. Rama took birth as prince of the ancient kingdom of Ayodhya, married Sita—the daughter of the famous enlightened king, Janaka—and destroyed the great demon Ravana, who had been harassing the three worlds. Rama is considered the incarnation of *dharma.*

Sadguru
A true Guru or spiritual teacher.

Sādhanā
The practice of spiritual discipline.

Saguna
Having attributes; the personal aspect of God.

Samādhi
Meditative union with the Absolute. *See also Ashtānga Yoga.*

Saura
One who worships the sun.

Shabda Brahma
Ultimate Reality in the form of thought-sound vibration; a state in which thought and word are identical.

Shaivite or Shaiva
One who worships the supreme Reality as Shiva; of, or relating to Shiva.

Shakti
Spiritual power; the divine Energy that creates, maintains, and dissolves everything in the universe.

Shaktipāt
(*lit.* the descent of grace) The transmission of spiritual power (Shakti) from the Guru to the disciple; spiritual awakening. *See also Kundalinī.*

Shiva
The all-pervasive supreme Reality, divine Consciousness; that aspect of God that represents the destruction of ignorance.

Shiva Sūtras
A Sanskrit text revealed to the ninth-century sage Vasuguptacharya. It is the scriptural authority for the philosophic school of Kashmir Shaivism.

Shri, Shree
A respectful title meaning beautiful or holy.

Shyam
A name of Lord Krishna.

Siddha
A perfected being; one who has attained mastery over the senses and their objects, and who lives in the state of unity-consciousness or enlightenment.

Siddha Yoga Meditation

A path to union of the individual with the Divine, which begins with *shaktipāt*, the inner awakening by the grace of a Siddha Guru. Swami Chidvilasananda is the living Master of this path. Siddha Yoga is the name Swami Muktananda gave to this path, which he first brought to the West in 1970.

Spanda Kārikās

One of the fundamental scriptures of Kashmir Shaivism. This collection of 53 verses composed by the ninth-century sage Vasuguptacharya describes how a yogi who remains alert can perceive the divine Principle in all of life.

Sushumnā Nādī

The central and most important of the channels of the subtle body, extending from the base of the spine to the top of the head. The *chakras* are situated in the *sushumnā*, and it is through the *sushumnā* that the awakened *kundalinī* energy rises. *See also Kundalinī; Nādīs.*

Swami

One who takes vows of renunciation in the Indian tradition; a monk.

Turīyātita

The state beyond the transcendental state; a supremely blissful state of complete freedom from all duality, permeated by the awareness of the one Self in all.

Upanishads

Ancient scriptures in the form of dialogues between sages and their disciples, which describe the nature of the Absolute and the means for attaining it. The central doctrine of the Upanishads is that the Self of a human being is identical to Brahman, the Absolute.

Vaikuntha

The abode of Lord Vishnu; heaven.

Vasuguptacharya

The ninth-century sage to whom Lord Shiva revealed the *Shiva Sūtras,* the scriptural authority of Kashmir Shaivism.

Vedanta

One of the six orthodox schools of Indian philosophy, exemplified by the Upanishads and other texts that consider the nature of the Self. Vedanta teaches that the universe is nothing but absolute Consciousness, within which the world—as we know it—is simply an appearance or reflection.

Vedas

Among the most ancient of the world's scriptures, the four Vedas are regarded as divine revealed, eternal wisdom. They are the *Rig Veda, Atharva Veda, Sāma Veda,* and *Yajur Veda.*

Yajñā

A sacrificial fire ritual in which various materials such as grains, spices, and ghee are offered in gratitude to the Lord, while Vedic mantras are chanted; a form of mental sacrifice.

Yamas and Niyamas

Restraints (*yamas*) and observances (*niyamas*) that are considered vital to one who is pursuing the yogic life. *See also Ashtānga Yoga.*

Yati

An ascetic or devotee.

INDEX

Advaita, 4

Ajapā-japa, 66-67

Ancestors, 15

Antahkarana, 31

Āsana(s), 5, 7, 17

Ashtānga yoga, 5, 54; *see also Yoga*

Astrology, 55-56

Ātman, 2-3, 14, 28, 29, 31-33, 39;
changelessness of, 61; functions of,
28-29; identity with Supreme
Self, 31-33; means of knowing, 3

Awakening, spiritual. *See Shaktipāt*

Ayodhya, 50

Bahinabai, 26

Bhagavad Gītā, 5, 6, 11, 31, 32, 33, 38,
48, 53, 63

Bhagiratha, 53

Bhakta, 8-10, 45, 49, 52; *see also* Devotion

Bhakti, 2, 8-11, 38, 40, 44, 45-51, 54-55,
65; and four bodies, 65; as path to
God, 2, 8-11; *see also* Devotion

Bhakti Sūtras, 10

Bhartrihari, 53

Bigotry, 26

Bliss, 8-9, 11, 20-21, 33, 36, 44-46, 48, 50-
51, 60-62, 78, 83; and *antahkarana*,
31; as an aspect of God, 29-30; and
the ego, 48; and fourth body, 66,
69; as goal of life, 2; bestowed by

Guru, 36; and *japa*, 53, 56, 58, 64,
66; and Kundalini, 16, 19, 23-24, 69;
nature of, 4; as object of yoga, 6-7

Body, 17, 31-33, 35, 47, 48; consciousness of, 22, 35; health and fitness
of, 6-8, 56; purification of, 17, 47,
48, 60; reactions of, to Shakti, 15; as
temple, 32; *see also* Four bodies

Brahma Sūtras, 2

Brahman, 4, 20, 25, 29-31, 35, 53-54, 56;
bliss of, 29, 30, 53; direct experience of, 13; Guru as visible form
of, 35, 37; indefinable nature of, 25,
50; light of, 65; realization of, 56;
saguna, 15

Chaitanya. See Consciousness

Chakras, 17, 23, 60; *see also* Kundalini

Chāndogya Upanishad, 36

Chanting, 10

Chiti, 14, 16-17, 19-20, 28-29, 61, 68-70, 79

Chiti shakti, 13-14, 68-69, 70; *see also*
Chiti; Shakti

Company, good and bad, 50

Concentration, 4-7, 21

Consciousness: pure, 2-4, 25, 28, 31, 68,
78-79; all-pervasiveness of, 16; as
Chiti Shakti, 13-14; and fourth
body, 76; as goal of life, 3; and
Guru, 20, 35-36; and mantra, 53, 57;
merging into, 3-6, 22, 53; self-limita-

95

tion of, 16; and *shaktipāt,* 17-18;
unchanging nature of, 68; *see also*
Chiti
Dasharatha, 50
Destiny. *See Karma*
Devotion, 23, 26, 40, 42, 54, 81, 82; to
Guru, 35, 37-38, 42, 44, 45-51, 79; of
Eklavya, 37, 40; of Gavba, 40-41; of
Giri, 37-38; of Jabala, 37, 40; and
mantra repetition, 56; path of, 8-11;
power of, 46-48; *see also Bhakta;*
Bhakti
Dhāranā, 5
Dhruva, 53
Dhyāna, 5, 7-8
Dīkshā, 11-14, 42; *see also Shaktipāt*
Discipleship, 38-44
Discipline, spiritual, 5-6, 11, 15-16, 19,
23, 55; *see also* Path, spiritual
Draupadi, 53
Dronacharya, 37, 40
Drik dīkshā. See Shaktipāt
Duality, 8, 33, 47-48, 81; *see also* Non-
duality
Eklavya, 37, 40
Eknath Maharaj, 34, 40-41
Four bodies, 76, 82; description of, 63-
64; and *japa,* 63-71
Fire, 19, 26, 28, 51; of desire, 39; of
knowledge, 33; of mantra, 65, 70;
seen in meditation, 20-21; of suf-
fering, 40; of yoga, 32, 43;
Gahininath, 12
Gheranda Samhita, 12
Giri, 37-38
God-realization. *See* Self-realization
Gopichand, 53
Goraknath, 53
Guru, -disciple relationship, 34-44;
grace of, 1-24, 28-33, 55, 66-68, 73-
75; inner, 75-77; love for, 45-51;
mantra given by, 54, 57-61, 66, 69;
nature of, 62; oneness with Consciousness of, 67-70; path of, 11-24,
31; teachings of, 3
Happiness, 1, 22, 26, 29, 50-51; attained

through mantra repetition, 55-57;
pursuit of, 1, 29-30, 48, 50; tran-
scending desire for, 45-46, 48
Hardship, 10, 66-67
Hastamalaka, 12
Heart, 10, 15, 18-20, 23, 26-28, 32-37, 72-
73, 75, 82; and causal body, 63-65;
and Guru, 36, 42, 45-51, 59, 62, 75;
japa in, 64-65; and Kundalini, 19, 22;
and love, 49; and mantra, 22, 59, 62
Householders, 7, 18, 44
Individual soul. *See Jīvātman*
Individuality, 3, 32, 36, 40, 67, 70
Initiation. *See Shaktipāt*
Īshwara Pratyabhijñā, 24
Jabala, 36-37, 40
Jaitrapal, 13
Janaka, 53
Japa, 53-58, 60, 64-65, 70-72, 75; breath
and, 60; four bodies and, 63-66;
Guru and, 62, 66-67; significance
of, 52
Japa yoga, 52-59, 63-64, 67
Jīvātman, 31-33, 63.
Jñāna, 40, 42, 54, 55, 65; *see also* Knowl-
edge
Jnaneshwar Maharaj, 34, 40
Jñāni, 4, 8, 11, 42, 52; *see also* Knowl-
edge
Kabir, 31, 34, 66; initiation of, 12
Kaikeyi, 50
Kali Yuga, 52
Kalpavriksha, 34, 56, 78
Kapilmuni, 6
Karma, 55-56, 67, 80-82
Katha Upanishad, 10
Knowledge, 2-4, 8, 11, 24, 28, 32, 50, 63,
67, 78; fire of, 33; of Guru, 36-37,
42, 46-47; and Kundalini, 23;
mantra and, 42, 52, 57, 59; path of,
72-83
Kriyās, 15-16
Kshemaraja, 2
Kulārnava Tantra, 12, 14
Kundalini, 18, 60; experiences of, 15,
22-24, 69; Guru and, 13-15, 19, 22;

shaktipāt and, 14
Liberation, 10, 48-49, 63, 67, 71; *see also* Self-realization
Life, 1, 3, 9, 27, 28, 30, 35, 43, 45, 47, 55-56, 60, 62, 71, 74, 81; daily, 7, 29, 44, 47, 50, 59; discipline and, 7-8; *see also* Worldly life
Light, divine, 28, 49, 72, 75; of Brahman, 15, 49, 65; of knowledge, 72; in meditation, 15, 21
Longing, 45, 48
Love, 12, 22-23, 25-27, 41-42, 44, 46-50, 56, 65, 79-80, 82; of God, 8-10; Guru and, 45-51; of others, 30
Maha Yoga, 21-23
Mahadeva, 27
Mahākārana, 67; *see also* Four bodies
Mahānirvāna Tantra, 57
Mahaprabhu, Chaitanya (Shri Gauranga), 12, 53
Mahāsamādhi, 41
Manana, 3
Manasa dīkshā, 12
Manpuri, 73
Manthara, 50
Mantra, 19, 42, 48, 51-58, 61, 70; breath and, 60; four bodies and, 63-66; Guru and, 59-60; Kundalini and, 60; as name of God, 52-53; as Word, 59; *see also Japa yoga*
Mantra japa, 58, 59, 62, 70
Mantrajata, 42
Mantravīrya, 42
Markandeya, 53
Meditation, 3, 7, 17, 27-28, 33, 37, 41-42, 74, 76, 83; experiences of, 15, 20-21; on the Guru, 43, 49-50, 69
Mind, 10, 24-25, 37, 45-47, 60-61, 69, 72, 83; attitude and, 79; and doubt, 35; Guru and, 48, 51; and *nāda*, 21; purification and, 21, 31-32, 45, 54; steadiness of, 4-7, 37, 49, 61, 66
Mira, 53
Moksha, 1; *see also* Self-realization
Moon, 16, 28, 30, 60, 65, 82
Mukundrai, 13

Music, inner, 21
Nāda, 21, 66
Nāma japa, 52-53, 56; *see also* Mantra; *Japa yoga*
Namdev, 53
Narada, 10, 53
Nature, 22-23; of the disciple, 38-44; of God, 9, 25-28, 30, 72, 82; of the Guru, 34-38; of the mantra, 56-63
Navel *chakra*, 65
Nididhyasana, 3
Nityananda, Bhagawan, 20, 26, 27, 32, 51, 69, 73, 74, 80, 81, 83
Nivrittinath, 12
Niyama, 5, 7-8
Nonduality, 47; *see also* Duality
Pairs of opposites, 4, 8, 79-82
Pashupata-brahma Upanishad, 15
Patanjali, Maharishi, 5-6
Path, spiritual, 2, 10, 25-27, 30, 35, 40-42, 54, 70; of concentration, 4-8; of devotion, 8-11; initiation into, 39-40; of knowledge, 2-4, 72; and mantra, 53-59; of the Siddhas, 11-24; *see also* Discipline, spiritual
Peace, 1, 21-25, 27, 30, 56, 73-75, 78-79
Prāna, 18-19, 59-60
Prānāyāma, 8, 17, 73
Pratyabhijñāhridayam, 32-33, 68
Pratyāhāra, 5
Prayer, 49, 53
Purification, 17, 32, 56
Purity, 22, 32, 35, 54, 80
Puranpolya, 41
Ramakrishna Paramahamsa, 12, 36
Sādhanā. See Discipline, spiritual; Path, spiritual
Saints: company of, 10; visions of, 21, 64
Samādhi, 5-7
Self. *See Ātman*
Self-realization, 1-2, 4, 10, 13, 31-35; and discipleship, 44; experience of, 22-24; and fourth body, 53, 70, 76; and grace, 32-33, 35; and knowledge, 72; and mantra, 53, 56-57, 70; and yoga, 70; *see also* Liberation

Senses, 10, 31, 48, 51, 61

Service, 10, 35-38, 44, 46, 77

Shakti, 12-14, 17-20, 22-24, 32, 43; and Shiva, 22, 23, 33, 60; unfolding of, 20, 24, 33, 43, 61; *see also Chiti shakti*

Shaktipāt, 11-14, 17, 42

Shankaracharya, 32, 54; and Hasta-malaka, 12; and Giri, 37-38

Shiva, 14, 18, 22, 69, 79; awareness of, 22, 24, 32-33, 60, 63, 67, 80; and Chiti, 68; and Guru, 43, 61-62; and Kundalini, 69; and mantra, 57-60; and Shakti, 22-23, 33, 60

Shiva Sūtras, 2, 16, 18-23, 34, 60, 69

Shrāvana, 3

Shrīmad Bhāgavata Purāna, 9

Shvetāshvatara Upanishad, 4

Siddhas, path of, 11-24

Siddhis, 44, 46, 55, 62

Skanda Purāna, 12

Sound, 57; God as, 58; Guru as, 51; as *nāda,* 21, 66; pervasiveness of, 57; primordial, 47

Spanda Kārikās, 18, 62

Speech, 28, 59, 66-67

Suffering, 1, 8, 38-39, 82

Surrender, 30, 36, 42

Taittirīya Upanishad, 9, 29, 31

Tandrā, 64-65

Tantrasāra, 17, 19

Throat region, 63-65

Tibet, 12, 69

Totakacharya, 38, 40

Upanishads, 2, 4, 9-10, 12, 15, 25, 29-31, 36

Vak yoga, 54

Vasuguptacharya, 62

Vedanta, 3-5, 29, 31, 33, 37-38, 63, 80-81

Vimarshini, 2, 16, 18, 20, 34

Visions, 17-18, 21, 64-65, 68

Vivekananda, Swami, 12, 36, 40

Vyasa, 6

Witness, inner, 75-76

Words, 4-5, 26, 30, 35, 59, 75; Guru's, 40, 77

World, creation of, 70; nature of 8-9, 14, 18-19, 29, 34, 36, 38, 46, 67-68, 70, 76-79, 81; other worlds, 15-16, 19, 82

Worldly life, 7-8, 18, 45, 50, 56, 59; *see also* Life, daily

Yajnavalkya, 6

Yajur Veda, 4

Yoga, 5-8; *see also Bhakti;* Discipline, spiritual; *Jñāna yoga;* Mantra; Path, spiritual

Yoga Sūtras, 5-6

Yoga Vāsishtha, 14

Yama, 5, 7-8

Ziapruanna, 74

FURTHER READING

by Swami Muktananda

Play of Consciousness
From the Finite to the Infinite
Where Are You Going?
I Have Become Alive
Nothing Exists That Is Not Shiva
The Perfect Relationship
Reflections of the Self
Secret of the Siddhas
I Am That
Kundalini
Mystery of the Mind
Selected Essays
Does Death Really Exist?
Bhagawan Nityananda of Ganeshpuri
Mukteshwari
Meditate
Conversations with Swami Muktananda

by Swami Chidvilasananda

Remembrance
Enthusiasm
The Yoga of Discipline
My Lord Loves a Pure Heart
Inner Treasures
The Magic of the Heart
Kindle My Heart
Ashes at My Guru's Feet

You may learn more about the teachings and
practices of Siddha Yoga meditation by contacting

SYDA Foundation
P.O. Box 600, 371 Brickman Rd.
South Fallsburg, NY 12779-0600, USA
Tel: (914) 434-2000

or

Gurudev Siddha Peeth
P.O. Ganeshpuri
PIN 401 206
District Thana
Maharashtra, India

For further information on books in print
by Swami Muktananda and Swami Chidvilasananda,
editions in translation, and audio and video recordings,
please contact

Siddha Yoga Meditation Bookstore
P.O. Box 600, 371 Brickman Rd.
South Fallsburg, NY 12779-0600, USA
Tel: (914) 434-2000 ext. 1700

Call toll-free from the United States and Canada: 888-422-3334
Fax toll-free from the United States and Canada: 888-422-3339